A VILLAGE OF
Knowledge

Retired Industry Leaders Coming
Together to Share Their Stories
Volume I

Author: Virginia Gean, MBA, CMA
Co-Author: Farrell Gean, PhD, MBA, CPA, CMA

authorHOUSE®

AuthorHouse™
1663 Liberty Drive
Bloomington, IN 47403
www.authorhouse.com
Phone: 1 (800) 839-8640

© *2018 Virginia Gean, MBA, CMA. All rights reserved.*

No part of this book may be reproduced, stored in a retrieval system, or transmitted by any means without the written permission of the author.

Published by AuthorHouse 09/19/2018

ISBN: 978-1-5246-4502-1 (sc)
ISBN: 978-1-5246-4503-8 (hc)
ISBN: 978-1-5246-4504-5 (e)

Library of Congress Control Number: 2018901312

Print information available on the last page.

Any people depicted in stock imagery provided by Getty Images are models, and such images are being used for illustrative purposes only. Certain stock imagery © Getty Images.

This book is printed on acid-free paper.

Because of the dynamic nature of the Internet, any web addresses or links contained in this book may have changed since publication and may no longer be valid. The views expressed in this work are solely those of the author and do not necessarily reflect the views of the publisher, and the publisher hereby disclaims any responsibility for them.

Contents

Dedication vii
Introductory Letter for *A Village of Knowledge*-"Gemstones of
Knowledge" by Blaine Shull ix
Introduction xi

Chapter 1   Robert James, Entrepreneur Extraordinaire-Sold
            his Company-Diaper Genie to Playtex for $120 Million ... 1
Chapter 2   John Shields, Trader Joe's-Former CEO and
            Builder of Trader Joe's Brand 21
Chapter 3   Steve Dorfman, Hughes Space and
            Communications-Former CEO, Contributed to
            Cable and Direct TV 41
Chapter 4   John Bardgette, Exxon-Former Executive, Former
            Senior Project Manager, 3 World Records 61
Chapter 5   Craig Zobelein, Hughes-Former Aerospace
            Engineer and 7 Other Careers 89
Chapter 6   Jennifer Zobelein-Author: *A Forest of Pipes*-Story of
            Disney Organ, Philanthropist and Teacher 117
Chapter 7   Peggy Perry, Volunteer, Teacher and Author 135

Acknowledgements 149
About the Authors 150

Dedication

The dedication of this book to Edward Young, Virginia's father, is more than an act of grace to a beloved parent and mentor. It is a renewed affirmation that this work could not have been created were it not for his encouragement and example over many years. His political prowess and entrepreneurial spirit led him to many noteworthy accomplishments. In so doing, he has been such a source of inspiration to us both. He has never allowed the pridefulness associated with his achievements to ripen into arrogance. This former United States Congressman may have silver in his hair but he has gold in his heart.

Introductory Letter for *A Village of Knowledge*-"Gemstones of Knowledge"

Blaine Shull, resident of University Village

Here at our university, we look across the street to a very attractive retirement community.
It is called University Village.
We glance at it daily, coming and going.
We had heard casual comments and hints about the people and activities going on over there.
Then, one recent morning as we glanced, we had a momentary vision of mountains there—mountains of experience.

Further talk suggested there just might be treasure buried in those mountains—enough talk that we decided to explore.
Then to prospect. Then to dig.
Dig we did, and we discovered treasures indeed. We struck gold!
The gold-enhanced gemstones!
Gemstones of experience. Gemstones of success. Gemstones of knowledge.

But how to mine these treasures?
Treasures in those mountains that were the homes of successful retired people.
Several hundred retirees live there.

All have done something very significant in their lives and have had a broad variety of careers, including:
aerospace, civil engineering, finance, investment banking, ministry, journalism, philanthropy, real estate, public relations, naval engineering, motion picture production, wealth management, pharmaceutical, and education, among others.
Potentially rich gemstone veins.

We mined by talking with and listening to many of the residents to learn of their backgrounds,
what they did, how they did it, and what lessons or core principles emerged from all of that experience.
Principles that may have come from bruises as well as successes.
What lessons did those wins and losses carry?

We made a most enlightening discovery: the residents identified and described what turned out to be significant *common* gemstone veins that run through all of those varied careers.

In this book, we have attempted to sort those veins into the basic gemstones of knowledge that resulted from the broad span of experiences.

The results are not mere platitudes. They are the down-to-earth, feet-on-the-ground, daily principles that are fundamental to success—the way you live, not just the way you talk.
The gemstones are here for the taking.
Look at them, examine them, think about them, and test them.
Then, *adopt* them. They will enhance your careers, or even make one.
Wear these gemstones on the inside. They will shine through for success.

Introduction

We never outgrow our love for a good story, do we? There is something compelling, something magnetic, and something altogether unique about the best stories. They engage both our minds and our hearts. They allow us to empathize with the experiences of other human beings. They also create opportunities to learn from the lives of others.

One can learn leadership qualities effectively by listening to the stories of those who have demonstrated successful leadership attributes in their careers. A group of such highly accomplished leaders lives at the same address in University Village located in Thousand Oaks, California. Collectively, these individuals possess a gold mine of leadership knowledge to be learned by anyone willing to listen.

Existence of this unique group led to a research project involving personal interviews of retired business leaders living in this location. Results of these interviews have been compiled for this book, which will be published in two volumes.

These successful leaders come from many different backgrounds and industries, but their messages are profoundly clear. Each urges aspiring leaders to live by the principles and values they share, and successful, fulfilling professional and personal lives will be achieved.

Volume 1 shares the stories of seven individuals who have lived at this address. The commonality of effective leadership qualities among these interviewees is remarkable. Here are a few nuggets from their interviews.

John Shields, former CEO and builder of the Trader Joe's brand, contends that leaders inspire and motivate others to realize their potential. True leaders are ethical. Leaders allow their people to make mistakes and learn from them. Leaders listen to their employees and their customers.

Leaders manage their time and energy well. Leaders have an innate sense of humor. Leaders articulate a clear vision of the goal.

Steve Dorfman, former CEO of Hughes Satellites and Communications, shares these aforementioned leadership qualities and provides more. Dorfman adds that a leader surrounds one's self with a team of smart people. Leaders show enthusiasm and gratitude. Leaders proactively look for opportunities to be seized with a positive attitude. Leaders recognize that they have been blessed with certain genetic endowments and should retain a sense of humility regardless of their successes.

A humble attitude was given a top priority by all interviewed. Willingness to work hard and willingness to take risks were two other attributes of successful leaders that permeated all the interviews.

Robert James, an entrepreneur extraordinaire, with multiple patents including the highly successful paper-wrapping machine, points to resiliency and flexibility along with many of the key attributes already identified by Shields and Dorfman. James contends that good leaders always have an exit strategy as they embrace new investments and projects. He notes the importance of using sound logic and reliable, empirical data to reduce excess risk.

John Bardgette, former Exxon executive and holder of multiple world records for building the largest oil platforms, agrees with Dorfman's emphasis on building successful teams. Likewise, he shares Shields's belief in the importance of empowering your employees and encouraging them with genuine sincerity. Bardgette, like so many others, maintained that integrity, honesty, and high ethical standards should govern your behavior to be an effective leader. Willingness to adapt policy and strategy as new information becomes available was another recurring critical leadership quality voiced by Bardgette and others.

In one way or another, each interviewee was saying, "Shout praise but whisper criticism," to all those you are attempting to lead. One of the most impressive attributes observed in all interviewees, without exception, is that in spite of their many noteworthy business leadership accomplishments, they have not allowed pride to ripen into arrogance.

Perhaps Blaine Shull, former Hughes Aircraft president of ground systems, expressed it best. Shull rather poetically describes the village as a vision of mountains of experience that should be mined. Mining would be listening to these successful residents. In so doing, the listener would learn how these leaders accomplished what they did and the lessons or core principles that emerged from their experiences.

If you want to appreciate fully the accomplishments of the seven leaders in volume 1 of this book, remove the halos from above their heads. Take away all of the aura—not all of the respect but all of the aura—that keeps you distant from Robert James, John Shields, Steve Dorfman, John Bardgette, Craig Zobelein, Jennifer Zobelein and Peggy Perry. Otherwise, you will hold them at such a distance that you will not see yourself in their lives. Take away all the glowing halos so you can see these individuals as people you can learn from and emulate.

Their stories can be your story. Their stories hold within them principles and insights and lessons that are timelessly significant. So whether you are boarding a plane, headed to the beach, resting in your favorite place for reading, or sitting in your dorm, it is time to open volume 1 of *A Village of Knowledge* and be informed, inspired, and entertained.

Chapter 1

Robert James, Entrepreneur Extraordinaire-Sold his Company-Diaper Genie to Playtex for $120 Million

The Life of an Entrepreneur
A Rags-to-Riches Story

Let's Get Ready to Talk about Tissue Paper and Diapers
Some Say It's a Tale about Tails!

Robert James

Virginia Gean, MBA, CMA

As one begins to ponder what the life of an entrepreneur would be like, one needs to look no further than the story of Robert James, entrepreneur extraordinaire. His is a life of humble beginnings. But through his rigorous belief in core principles, James was able to overcome his poverty and a lack of formal education—which ended at the age of thirteen during the London Blitz in World War II—to have a life of significant wealth. You might ask yourself, *Just how was he able to create a fortune from such meager beginnings?* This chapter will tell the story of this extraordinary human being who was born in the East End of London in 1925.

Before we travel through his life, let's fast forward to a few of his major achievements in business and focus on a few of the colleagues and clients that he has worked with—names with which we are all familiar. His impressive list of clients includes dozens of nationally and internationally recognized leaders, from Frito-Lay, Proctor & Gamble, and Scott Paper Company to the London Underground. He sold one company, Diaper Genie, to Playtex Inc., for $120 million. James has over forty US patents with hundreds of foreign analogues.

Let's take a close look at one of the products in the beginning stages of his entrepreneurial career. Again, something we're all familiar with—toilet tissue.

Some products may often get overlooked, but business is everywhere. Take James, who at one point counted juggernaut Proctor & Gamble and Scott Paper as clients. How did he do this? By wrapping individual packages of toilet tissue in the two-, four-, six-, eight-, ten-, twelve-, and twenty-four-pack configurations common in supermarkets today. The four-roll pack was produced at three hundred packs per minute.

James's fortune is rooted in the transformation, innovation, and continuous improvement of the sanitary-paper-packaging industry. Shopping down the aisles of supermarkets, one can see the results and the actual products that James produced over a lifetime. In fact, his paper-packaging machines still produce 80 to 90 percent of the sanitary tissue packaging worldwide. To put this into perspective, imagine that 80 to 90 percent of the individual toilet tissue currently being sold throughout the world is produced on the machines that James created and engineered in his lifetime. Staggering, isn't it?

He pioneered much of this engineering technology, which led to the sale of several of his patents and the sale of companies that he created to such conglomerates as International Paper and Playtex Inc.

James became more diversified. With five partners, each investing $200,000, he started a company known as Diaper Genie. That endeavor became another big success for him and the investors, and only seven years later, as previously mentioned, they sold the company to Playtex Inc. for $120 million.

James recalled the renaissance of the successful enterprise: "Six of us got together, and in 1990, we formed a company called Diaper Genie, which created a sanitary method of disposing of soiled baby diapers individually," James said. "It was a brand-new product category, and we built a new factory to produce this product. In the first year, we got all of our money back, and we finally sold it seven years later to Playtex Inc."

Still, James conceded that all that money wasn't put in the investors' pockets. They did have to pay the bank back. Nonetheless, the company hit a home run.

The product was a free-standing, cone-shaped, plastic container. A replaceable cartridge containing a plastic tube was placed in the top of the big container, and voilà, a sanitary method of individually disposing of soiled baby diapers was achieved.

To understand James's path to success from living in poverty in London back in the 1920s to becoming a wealthy man, we will trace the path of his life and the multiple decisions that he made along this journey. In his own humble way, James will often mention that it was simply luck that took him down certain paths. However, it is clear that his success was certainly based on much more than luck. It was based on important concepts and principles that he discovered from childhood and applied throughout adulthood. These core principles were life lessons that James learned, discovered, and carefully nurtured as he matured and business became such a big part of his life. As a young child and throughout his adolescence, he did not have a conceptual framework for business success. However, it would become solidified as he gained more and more experience in business, and it began to emerge and crystallize during his adult life.

Those core principles that James discovered would become the guiding concepts that enabled him to achieve such success in business. These core principles, as building blocks for the success he enjoyed, would be developed and used as a parallel to his personal life as he grew from a young child to the present. There is an interesting correlation between these principles and his career as he developed his skills as an entrepreneur and his journey throughout his life. James identified the key concepts as follows.

Resiliency and Flexibility

From a Young Childhood to Early Adulthood

James was born in 1925 in the East End of London. He left school at age thirteen in 1939. He remembers the time precisely. It was the beginning of the summer, and within a few months, World War II would begin.

"There was no schooling because the probability of the war was known, and on September 3, when war was declared on Germany, a lot of the children, myself included, were evacuated out of London because everybody expected London to be bombed to hell and back immediately," James said.

If you ask James to tell you about his life, he may wittingly respond with a question of his own: "Would you like the fifty-cent version or the one-dollar-and-fifty-cent version?"

James, along with many of London's citizens, began to drift back to London in late 1939 due to the fact that the Blitz didn't start until the summer of 1940. After his return to London, there was no schooling, and therefore, his formal education was over. So James decided to look for a job, and he was able to take on a job as an apprentice toolmaker. He continued as an apprentice toolmaker for nearly four years. This became the foundation for his future career, as it taught him important engineering principles and the ability to manufacture them.

Volunteerism for Greater Opportunity

Early Adulthood in the British Royal Air Force

Being a volunteer began the path that would exemplify the flexibility and resilience of Robert James. He understood the constraints of not having an education and believed that he could make a better life for himself through volunteerism. He knew that by volunteering before he turned eighteen, he could ask for the branch of service and the specific job within that branch of service that he most wanted. If he had waited until the age of eighteen and been drafted, James knew he could have been placed into any of the other armed services. So he was soon inducted and got his wish to be a part of the Royal Air Force. At age eighteen, in early 1943, he was called up and trained for the next eighteen months to become a Spitfire pilot. James flew as a bomber escort, though the war ended in July 1945. Britain's postwar policy was to keep their military in place and release them according to length of service so that the war veterans would not flood the job market. James continued to work in the Royal Air Force for two years as a manager heading up a motor transit group. While American veterans had the GI Bill—legislation that was passed in 1944 in the United States that gave veterans a wide range of benefits, such as cash payments for tuition to college, high school, or vocational school and living expenses, as well as low-cost loans or low-cost mortgages—British soldiers didn't have those opportunities. After demobilization, James had to look for conventional employment.

Innovate through Research and Development

From Waxed Paper to Cellophane: Patents and Innovation

From Toolmaker to the Military to Entrepreneur: His First Big Break

After his deployment with the Royal Air Force, James again sought employment. Since he had prior experience as a toolmaker, he decided to continue in that trade.

"I was demobilized from the military, and I got a job with a company called British Cellophane, and that was a division of Courtaulds, Ltd. This was a large company, which still exists. It's much like the DuPont Company, a huge conglomerate," he said. "In 1947, I was hired as a technical service engineer, and my job was to go to all of the manufacturers of machinery that handled paper, printing it, making it into bags, overwrapping cartons, to be sure that they knew what they had to do to adapt their machines to handle cellophane."

Prior to James's involvement, many machines were designed to wrap using waxed paper. Bread, along with many other items, was wrapped in waxed paper for mass distribution. James had the responsibility of assuring all wrapping machines were designed to handle cellophane. Furthermore, he contended that they could not expand the use of cellophane unless there was a large population of machines in the field capable of using this material.

And James is not bashful in asserting his role in the growth of the sector. "I helped build the market," he said.

The history of British Cellophane is quite interesting, as James assisted British Cellophane and their customers toward innovation and toward the transition from waxed paper, which was previously used, to the newer, stronger, and better material of cellophane, for packaging. Through innovation, the equipment to produce this new cellophane material also had to be reengineered from the use of waxed paper to cellophane.

British Cellophane Factory

A Village of Knowledge

British Cellophane Factory

In 1937, British Cellophane set up production on a site in Bridgwater, when unemployment levels in the town were high. The new buildings covered fifty-nine acres of the former Sydenham Manor fields and had direct railway access. The factory produced cellophane up until late 1940, when it started switching production to war munitions and specifically Bailey bridges for the pending invasion of Europe. These were first used in Italy in 1943 by the Royal Engineers. Production ramped up through early 1944 for D-Day. After the war, the Bridgwater factory returned to producing cellophane, with its products exported globally.

In 1957, a secondary facility was started at Barrow in Furness in Lancashire (now in Cumbria). A subsidiary, Colodense Ltd. of Bedminster, Bristol produced special cellophane printed and colored bags for food packaging in supermarkets. James was successful in that enterprise, developing a couple of patents in the UK. Eventually the company decided to set up a manufacturing operation in Canada. "I was asked if I would go over to Canada and become a technical service manager. So I talked to my wife, we had one son at that time, and asked her if she would like to emigrate," James recalled. "I could not wait to get there, and she was all for it, and so we emigrated, and that was in April of 1952. If I look back at 1952 in the UK at that time, things were very, very difficult. The country had no money, and all of its finances had been used up to buy weapons and to help with the war effort."

So James and his family arrived in Montreal, which he thought was a wonderful city. After about two years, James decided that British Cellophane was a dead-end career choice. It was such a large company, and with no educational background, he felt there was no upward mobility. "In those days, if you had not gone to Oxford or Cambridge, or similar universities, you really did not stand a chance," James said.

He decided to move on but was unsure about what the next step would be. Perhaps luck would intervene. James recalled talking to a man he had done some business with in Montreal. He was a manufacturer and importer of packaging machines, some of which handled cellophane, and his name was Howard Griswold. James told his colleague he didn't know what to do next but that he didn't want to stay with British Cellophane. On the spot, Griswold offered him a job as a sales manager.

"Within two years, I was able to double sales for that business," James said. "One day, he came to me and he said, 'Bob, this business is getting too technically complicated for me. I have another business up in Toronto, and I would like to move up there with my family, and I want you to buy the business from me.'"

Opportunity had knocked, and James was eager to answer. He jokingly offered $500 for the business. Griswold knew James had no money, so the two arranged a ten-year buyout program, by which James would pay off the business out of the profits that were generated.

In about 1954, business was booming in Canada, and James said he was able to pay Griswold off within two years. "I doubled the business in the next year, and again I doubled it in the next year," James said. What was the business? Packaging machinery.

Listen to the Needs of Your Customers to Understand the Marketplace

And Thus Increase Sales for Your Business

Robert James's First and Second Big Breaks

This progression in James's career path, from impoverished and humble beginnings to an apprentice toolmaker, British Spitfire pilot, and now to owning a packaging machinery business in the year of 1956, was quite extraordinary. He was only thirty at this point in time. His career continued to grow and accelerate as he became more and more intrigued with innovation, research and development, and the reengineering of packaging machinery. He went on to explain that being a tradesman in the tool-making business was a very valuable apprenticeship for the packaging machinery business. James said it was a good foundation for understanding the packaging business and being able to innovate and improve this complicated machinery. This would help James create important patents that would eventually be sought out by many important companies. He described several instances of patent creation, which ultimately would lead to increased revenue and profit for his newly acquired business.

But how was he able to double his business and then again double the business within only a few short years? James gets excited about telling the story of building his business. "Well, there is an old saying. It's the man who makes the calls that gets the business," he said. "So you get out, you knock on doors, and you get rejected, and you go knock on doors again." This is a story of the fundamental importance of understanding your product, the technology, and most importantly, listening to the needs of your customers.

He went on to say, "If you don't know your product, you absolutely cannot sell it, and people soon find that out." Obviously, James knew his product, since he helped to develop it and had the patents to prove it.

In 1957, James invented a machine for using corrugated cardboard—a machine still used today for corrugated cartons. This corrugated cardboard comes in a blank, and the carton is set up around the products, and the flaps are folded and sealed. What James did, and this has to be for very high production, was he took the open blank before it is made into a carton and folded it around the product, folding the sides, then sealing it. You could get more blank cartons onto the machine because if it is folded together, it doubled the thickness. Secondly, if you fold it around the product that you want to ship, it makes a very tight package. And a tight package is much more protective than a loose one. The concept went so swimmingly that the biggest paper company in the world, International Paper, came to James looking for a deal.

"They wanted to buy the patent. I thought about selling the patent, but I said that I really did not want to sell the patent," James said. "But I told them that if they wanted to buy the whole company, that was possible."

Look for the Big Break; Embrace It, Leading to an Exit Strategy

James said the reason he wanted to sell the company to International Paper instead of selling only the patent was twofold. Firstly, James said he knew that he would have had to go to the bank and borrow a lot of money to continue to grow the business and to build a new factory, because the existing one was too small. Secondly, at that time, Canada had no capital gains tax. There was a lot of talk about it as the United Kingdom, Britain had just put one in, so if James sold the company, all of the dollars were his, and nothing went to the Canadian government. International Paper bought the company in early 1960, just three years after the patent was first issued. "So at that point, I had made enough money to retire," James said. "I was only thirty-five years of age."

And how much could James get for a company he had bought from Howard Griswold only a few years prior? Ten million dollars.

The Importance of Risk Management Used With Logic

James was not only extremely intelligent from an engineering and marketing perspective, without any formal education, but also showed brilliance in his ability to understand that it would be better to sell his company to International Paper rather than just his patent. He knew from a risk management perspective that it would be incredibly risky for him to borrow millions of dollars to build a new and larger manufacturing factory for packaging machinery. James saw an exit strategy in selling the business to International Paper for $10 million, and he gladly took it. The capital would enable him to take the cash as all his, due to the lack of capital gains taxes in Canada. Having this tremendous amount of cash in early 1960 would further allow him to have the liquidity required to expand into new and more diversified businesses with a lower risk. James said he called it "my go-to-hell fund." From this point forward, James would have adequate capital for new and greater projects throughout the rest of his business life.

"The deal with International Paper was so great that I could not turn it down. I have a high tolerance for risk, but it has to be backed up with some segment of logic and data," James said. "I would not go to a casino, because I cannot control the odds. You just have to have some logic to back it up."

He also explained the ultimate demise of his factory that he sold to International Paper. James said the company, being based in New York, did not pay the operation the attention it deserved. "I would have stayed on at the company if they had asked me to, either on the board or to continue to run the company with a salary as an employee," he said. "However, they said no, they knew better, and they had to put their own people in and run it their own way." International Paper bought the company because it was successful, but then they turned it over to their people, who didn't not know anything about the business, according to James. And within seven years, the company was down the drain, and the factory was shut down.

"I watched it go down from a distance, and there was nothing that I could do," James said. "I just knew a number of the people from the lower echelon of the company who stayed on, and I stayed in touch with them, and they kept me informed about the progress and the ultimate demise of the company."

Many large companies make acquisitions and don't really understand the business, the customer, or the needs of the customer. That's not even counting that they do not know how to manage the business from an engineering, technological, or technical approach. International Paper did not recognize that the original success of the company was largely based on the vision, imagination, and inspiration of a leader such as James. So within a seven-year period, International Paper had spent $10 million on a factory that ultimately went out of business, largely due to a lack of leadership.

Use Leadership and Strategy to Empower Your Employees

Almost immediately after James sold his business, he received a call from a man in Wisconsin with whom he had worked considerably as a supplier of wrapping machinery. The man was in the packaging machinery business. His father had started the business in 1910, and it was 1960 when he called James. He was in the hospital, recovering from a heart attack, and his wife had been given eighteen months to live because she had been diagnosed with cancer. He asked James if he could come be the general manager during this difficult time in his life. The man's name was Bill Hayssen. Additionally, Hayssen was building a new factory on forty acres of land and wanted to continue to be the general contractor, since he was not needed there every day doing the daily chores. The packaging machinery company at that time was doing about $3 million in sales per year.

So James moved his family from Canada to Sheboygan, Wisconsin, which was a very, very quaint Midwestern town. He considered it a great place to raise his children. The people that worked for James were third-, fourth-, and fifth-generation German immigrants. Some of the people in this Wisconsin community still spoke German and very little English at that time. "When I took over the factory, I often had sons, fathers, and grandfathers all working in the factory," James declared with a look of amusement. "The average wage was $1.10 per hour."

When James arrived, he already knew what the company needed from representing them earlier in Canada. They needed the machinery to perform the same function but at higher speeds, and he knew what to do to get the higher speed. Upon examining the equipment, he observed that the machines that they were building were operating at thirty-five packages a minute. He knew it was critical to go faster, so he set as a first objective that in the next one hundred days, these machines must run one hundred packages a minute. He stressed to the employees that this objective must be top priority. These were overwrapping machines for things like loaves of bread, cigar boxes, and multipacks of cigarettes. The company built the machinery and shipped them to the customers who were manufacturing various products.

One of the big products that was coming along at that time was copy paper. And so a ream of paper was something else the company was able to wrap. The company started in 1910 wrapping bread, and the bread was wrapped in waxed paper, and then it was relatively easy to transfer that to cellophane. James said he came to the conclusion that the bread-wrapping business was not a good business to be in because there were no more small bakeries.

"The big, multiple outlet bakeries were only interested in price, price, price, price, and price," James said. "And if you weren't in with them, you were not anywhere."

So rather than developing a high-speed bread-wrapping machine, James developed machines for the packaging of toilet tissue, household towels, and paper napkins in cellophane. Because polyethylene was coming in, he was able to adapt and switch to plastic. "That sounds easy, but it was a totally different technique from cellophane to plastic," he said.

In fact, if you go into any supermarket and buy any toilet tissue or household towel, James said 90 percent of it is done on his machines. So if you walk into a Costco, Wal-Mart, or any supermarket to get toilet tissue, from the four-roll pack to the gigantic wrapped package, it is more than likely produced on a Robert James machine.

"Proctor & Gamble was one of my clients, along with Scott Paper and Fort Howard Paper," he said. "In fact, all of the people in sanitary tissue business all over the world were my clients." And so James's radical ideas on how to ramp up and triple production paid off. James said he never went to employees and told them what they had to do but instead focused on motivating them with the thought that this level of production was something they could do, and it would help their long-term job security.

"It established me and cemented me as a leader for the new company. However, I did not own it at the time," James said with great enthusiasm. "Well, you have to do something a little bit more than just saying you are going to be doing one hundred packages per minute in one hundred days. You have to have some idea of how to get there."

All the existing machines in those days were all mechanical, with few exceptions, such as electric motors and heaters to heat seal. He knew that the way that the existing machines were feeding the film took half a cycle of the operation. He knew there was a competitor that had a sixty-a-minute machine, and they had had it for a long time. So James got the engineering department together and told them to change all of the designs of the cams on the assumption that the film could be fed in a quarter of a cycle and not half of a cycle. James actually purchased a competitor's used machine to get started.

"I bought it from a used machinery dealer. I took off the film feed end of it and jerry-rigged it to fit the existing machine with the reworked cams," James said. "In about sixty days, we were actually wrapping at one hundred units per minute."

James's gift for leadership, his innovation in engineering, and the patents that he had created enabled him to gain the respect and support of the employees within the organization. If employees see you as someone who knows what you are doing and has done it successfully in the past, they have respect—and that gave James credibility.

Then there is the issue of marketing to consider.

"You have got to be very close to your customers to find out what their future needs might be," he said. "You can invent and design the best machine in the world, and if there is no place for it, what is the value in that? This happened in the case of bread wrapping. Within a year or so, the industry switched from wrapping to premade plastic bags. Bread is sold that way today. The best place to get that is not just from the marketing department of Proctor and Gamble or Scott Paper, but you have got to get to the people closer to the top." And James was able to do that.

After James and his firm had reached that goal of one hundred packages per minute, still using the competitor's infeed, he took that off and totally reengineered it. The competitor's machine was from a company called Package Machinery Company out of East Long Meadow. James was able to apply for a new patent for his new machine, which was subsequently granted.

"It taught us a lot about feeding film in a different way. The first one of these one-hundred-unit machines I sold to Heinz Company located in Canada for wrapping their cartons of baby formula." Then in 1966, the man who owned the company decided to sell it, and James jumped at the chance.

Earlier in 1962, James formed a company in the UK to produce the same machines, because no European money could be exchanged for US dollars at that time; however, there was a pent-up demand. In 1964, for similar reasons, he opened up a company in Italy.

"A lot of the European countries were demanding the machines be to metric standards. Because we needed distribution in Europe, I started a sales and service operation in France and Germany," he said. James clearly had an international presence.

Robert James Grows His Business into an International Enterprise

Standards for Manufacturing Are Critical to Success

In 1970, James took over a company in Austria, which he ruefully admitted was not a good thing to do, since it was out of his sphere of competence. The company manufactured twin screw extruders for unplasticized PVC to make floor tile and pressure pipe. All of their business was behind the Iron Curtain, and it was difficult to do business in a communist country. One of the things that James inherited was a commitment to build two factories—one in Moscow and one in Leningrad.

"At one time, I had ninety service engineers in Russia, and they were installing machines and building the factories," he said. "Every Friday night or Saturday night, I would get a call advising that two or three of them had had too much vodka and they were in jail."

This was taking place during the Cold War era, and while James described the experience as "kind of fun," it was certainly not business friendly. When expanding into international markets, it is more critical than ever to confirm the quality of your customer supplier of raw materials. This is important when working only within domestic borders but becomes more of a risk when having to use raw materials from an unknown source.

Before James had taken over the Austrian firm, a contract for manufacturing PVC floor tile for Russia had already been written. James had no input into the written contract. There were some guarantees that needed to be agreed on in order to get the contract. The Russians wanted guarantees of performance for the PVC floor tile, and to get the contract, these had been agreed to. Unfortunately, when it came time to test the equipment, the performance standards stipulated in the contract were not achieved.

James learned an important lesson when he went to Moscow, following up on this failed performance. It was determined that the reason the performance test failed was that Russian PVC had been used. And it did not behave anything like Western PVC.

Negotiations followed. James argued that their numbers were based on Western PVC and were very conservative. James proposed to import twenty tons of Western PVC and put it into production. Furthermore, he contended that with his service engineers and the newly acquired Western PVC, which he would furnish, he would process the twenty tons and prove to the Russians that he could exceed the performance guarantees that were in the contract.

James told the Russians that he expected them to pay for the twenty tons if standards were met, and if not, then he would pay for the twenty tons. Interestingly, James said, "Never did they say, 'Well what if that doesn't work, what you are going to do?' We shipped in the twenty tons, and our guys ran it, and it far exceeded the expectations," he said. "I never heard another word from them, and they just accepted it. It seems one generalization about the Russians is that once they sign on the dotted line, there is never any problem of payment." The lesson that James learned is not to expect all raw materials to behave the same from different sources.

James has and continues to do a lot of business in Japan. He is on the board of a company now in Milwaukee that ships product from Milwaukee to China and to India. This is very special material for the flooring for buses and trains. Its claim to fame is that it is a lightweight product, which is important today because of energy use. It is also fire proof, which none of the existing systems are. This is flooring, not floor tile, but flooring that you stand on in the train. Presently, here and in Europe, floors are made of a sandwich of plywood with a stainless surface on top and bottom. The company has obtained a patent on a process for embedding an electrical element in the flooring, so that when you get into the train or the bus, instead of having the hot air blowing from the sides, you put your feet on the floor, and it will be nice and warm. This is radiant heat that comes up through the floor.

James is also on the board of another company in Milwaukee that makes special membrane switches. When you go to the gas pump or your microwave and push the buttons, those are membrane switches. The first company name is Milwaukee Composites Inc., and the other is XYMOX Technologies Inc. Sales are relatively small at both firms, with James putting sales of approximately $20 million a year per company.

In Milwaukee Composites, the sales in China and India represent approximately 10 percent of overall sales revenue but are growing. They are currently exporting to Canada and the UK. If you go on the London

Underground, or the Toronto Subway, or the BART system in San Francisco, they are all using the Milwaukee Composites Inc. flooring product. There is little doubt that the company has increased its international presence.

James is no longer in the packaging industry and said, "When I retired out of the packaging business and sold the company, I had operations in the UK, France, Germany, Italy, and four factories in the US. So I retired at age sixty-five, and after a while, I started four more companies, one which was very, very successful."

At eighty-nine, James continues to work and is active, still contributing to society through manufacturing diversified products throughout the world. What drives a man like this?

"Well it is important to keep your brain active, no matter what age you are," he said, pointing to his head. "If you don't keep this going … well, I do not want to find out what would happen."

Recognize a Dud When You See One and Get Out!

The Starbucks Coffee Cup Story

No entrepreneur or successful business person has gone through a career without some duds. And James certainly has quite the dud story to tell. And that dud was his invention of the replacement for the Starbucks coffee cup. This turned out to be a dud, but as soon as he recognized it for being so, he intuitively backed out of pursuing this opportunity.

"A friend and myself came up with a double-walled cup with an air gap between them," James said. This formed a layer of insulation and eliminated the need for the serendipitous Java Jacket. "We went up to Starbucks's head office in Seattle and met with the executives twice. The people that we met with were very excited because it was the same cost as the existing cup, but it eliminated the cost of the Java Jacket. We came close to signing a contractual agreement with Starbucks, but then at the last minute, we were turned down, which made absolutely no sense to us. There was obviously some senior management intervention in the project."

Starbucks is still using the cup with the Java Jacket, and so that was a dud for James. "Since we could not get into Starbucks, we decided that it would be too much of an uphill battle to continue with the project."

Five Self-Proclaimed Principles for Success, in James's Own Words

1. **Role of Luck**
   "I have to go back and tell you that I am a great believer in luck. I think that is pretty important because things are presented to people, and maybe they make a lucky decision or maybe they make an unlucky decision. But if I look back through my life, all things are a crossroad where you can go one way or another; it is luck that takes you down the right one." This credit reference to Lady Luck seems to be an outgrowth of his humility. It is an attempt to downplay his abilities and demonstrates the lack of an ego.

2. **Recognizing That You Have Options**
   "The second principle would be to recognize that you have options. I talked about coming to the fork in the road and taking the right one. Now that could be luck or that could be perceived as being receptive to different options. I have seen a lot of people who have had luck presented to them, what I call luck, and they have said, 'No, I don't want to do that.'"

3. **Having a High Tolerance for Risk**
   "I have a high tolerance for risk, but it has to be backed up with a segment of logic and data. I would not go to a casino, because I cannot control the odds. You just have to have some logic in back of it."

4. **The Importance of People and Team Building**
   "If I go back to the people who have helped me during my life and have been very kind to me, and in a way helping themselves as well, I cannot thank them enough. It is important to note that I could not have accomplished what I did without them. It is essential to have the right people to support you, but you must earn their respect and trust. This is the essence of having the enthusiasm and team building as being essential to a successful business."

5. **The Importance of Innovation—Research and Development**
"I am a great believer in hands-on. I spent a lot of my time in the research and development department. In fact, I would go in on a Saturday and Sunday and work in the R&D department, without anyone around, so that I could really think and act. In fact, I would take my kids to the factory on a Saturday or a Sunday when they were learning to drive, and they would go around the parking lot, driving and parking and parallel parking while Dad was in the office working. When I started off, I used to say if it didn't have cams, gears, sprockets, and chains, it would never work. When I left, all of the machines were driven by several DC motors that were all coordinated through a programmable controller."

Still Kickin'

James also started a company with his three sons—an investment firm. James said he started the company just as a way to keep his sons together even after he's gone.

"One lives in Thousand Oaks, one lives in Wisconsin, and one lives in Florida," he said. "I want them to stay connected not with just telephone calls but like adhesive. We have investments now in nine different companies, and it is very successful, and they love it. This is the adhesive to keep them together."

His sons manage the company and make all of the crucial decisions on where to invest. The firm looks at manufacturing companies with annual sales from $5 to 20 million. James said if he could start all over again, he would focus more heavily on finance.

"I am very good at P&L, profit and loss statements, but I am not so good at reading a balance sheet," he said. "I know that if you make a profit all of the time, then the balance sheet is going to take care of itself."

James casually stood up, eager to thank his next-door neighbor for a fruit basket he had delivered last week. "I think you will recognize his name," James said with a smile. "John Shields, retired CEO of the well-known food store chain Trader Joe's. And does he have a wonderful life story to tell.

"That's a wrap!"

Robert James: Key Concepts for Business Success

1. Resiliency and flexibility.
2. Volunteerism for greater opportunity.
3. Innovation through research and development.
4. Listen to the needs of your customers, present and future, to understand the marketplace and thus increase sales for your business.
5. Use leadership and strategy to empower your employees.
6. Look for the big break and embrace it, leading to an exit strategy, which ties into risk tolerance, but use logic and data to reduce excess risk.
7. Recognize luck, which will take you down critical paths (this may represent James's humility); credit to others takes him off of center stage.

Chapter 2

John Shields, Trader Joe's-Former CEO and Builder of Trader Joe's Brand
Retired CEO of Trader Joe's
The Stages of Life of a Retail Giant

From Trader Joe's in Its Infancy to a Multibillion-Dollar Conglomerate

John Shields

Virginia Gean, MBA, CMA

Trader Joe's in the Infant Stages of Life—The Micromanager

One of the people in the village Robert James is most fond of is John Shields, who he said often brings him gifts from Trader Joe's. Shields, his next-door neighbor, was once the chief executive officer of this well-known grocery enterprise.

It does not take long to discover after speaking to Shields that he is indeed another resourceful human being who has achieved extraordinary accomplishments. John Shields spent his whole career in the retail sector, eventually leading the Trader Joe's grocery chain from its meager beginnings of six stores and seven hundred employees to over two hundred stores with sales exceeding $5 billion per year. This is another incredible tale of a leader of epic proportions, and another leader who lives alongside all of his neighbors at University Village, an intellectual, community think tank.

Shields and James are not only close neighbors but also share many of the same ideas when it comes to business strategy. He said many of the residents of this unique village mention to him regularly that they are customers and love the food, the beautiful orchids, and the myriad products the chain offers. But Shields recalls a time when the grocer wasn't quite the household name it is today.

As he reminisced, Shields explained that his entry as president and CEO of the company did not exactly begin smoothly. He described the somewhat rocky and unpredictable paths that led him into this leadership role, which were quite interesting.

Shields began his retirement after working for several large retail chains for more than twenty-nine years. He retired at the age of fifty-five. Shields said that out of nowhere, he received a phone call from Joe Coulombe, his fraternity brother from Stanford University, where they both attended graduate business school. Coulombe called Shields to ask him what he was currently doing. Shields responded by saying he was doing nothing at all since retiring. Coulombe asked to meet his old friend for lunch the next day at the Pasadena Cal Tech Faculty Club.

Shields mentioned that Coulombe seemed to be melancholy, and after inquiring about his mood, Coulombe explained that he believed the company that he founded could not grow over six stores. He went on to say that he had previously sold this company, Trader Joe's, to a German family seven years prior. Coulombe also told Shields that he was considering advising the German family to sell the small grocery business.

However, Coulombe was not ready to throw in the towel yet, and knowing that Shields had an extensive career in retail, first as an executive at Macy's department store for twenty years and then an executive at Mervyn's, which had been recently acquired by Dayton Hudson nine years prior to his retirement, Coulombe asked him if he would like to come to Trader Joe's and help manage and expand the business. At first thought, Shields believed it wouldn't be too difficult since he had the experience of growing both Macy's and Mervyn's into huge department chains nationwide. Coulombe asked Shields if he would be interested in coming out of retirement to take a month or two to analyze the business and flesh out some of the opportunities that might exist to increase the Trader Joe's business.

Shields agreed to do so and performed his research primarily by talking to managers, supervisors, and employees. He conducted extensive interviews over the course of several months. He talked with practically everyone in the company. Shields further explained that Coulombe was a micromanager. Coulombe would usually hire his employees right out of high school and therefore think of them as being children.

"Once you have that concept in your mind, you would not want to empower your children to do that much," Shields said of Coulombe's management style. After extensive analysis of the SWOTS, or the strengths and weaknesses of the company, Shields called Coulombe and asked him if he would like to meet again to discuss his analysis of Trader Joe's.

While discussing his analysis, Shields began to communicate his impression of Coulombe's management style as being one of the primary obstacles in the growth of the company. Shields said that he believed the company could grow but not the way Coulombe was managing it. He called Coulombe a "kind of micromanager."

As Shields burst out laughing, he further described his conversation with Coulombe, who immediately asked Shields what he meant by "micromanager." Shields went on to say that Coulombe was making every decision in the company and giving employees titles that did not translate to any real responsibility.

Shields further explained that though he hesitantly said those words, he had to speak from his heart. Shields also described that there were absolutely no training programs for people or anything like that to develop people and their management skills at the Trader Joe's Company. After that heart-stopping conversation, Shields went away thinking that he had destroyed Coulombe's confidence and wondered if he had gone too far in his criticism of his friend's management style. As lunch ended, they parted ways, and Shields had a moment where he thought he might not ever hear from his Stanford fraternity brother again.

In hindsight, Shields had hoped that he had not been too abrupt. But as he thought about it, he felt that it would be better to be honest than to soft-pedal his opinion. Shields was using a "micro master" label since he believed Coulombe had been issuing directives to his employees that must be obeyed. Overall, Shields had mixed emotions about the outcome of their luncheon conversation and was unsure about the future management opportunity at Trader Joe's.

Two weeks rolled by without Shields hearing from Coulombe, and his suspicions seemed to be coming to fruition. However, at the end of the second week, he got a call from Coulombe, who said, "Congratulations, my friend. I want you, John Shields, to be the new president, and I will be the chairman of Trader Joe's." They agreed to do just that, and after one year, Coulombe retired from the company, and John Shields became the CEO of Trader Joe's grocery store chain.

Trader Joe's in the Shakeup of Management Stages of Life—The Phew Factor

Shields reflects back to the time when he worked in retail at Macy's and Mervyn's. During his thirty years of working as an executive at those companies, he often wonders what he would do differently if he had the opportunity to be the CEO. Then, with this newly minted position as top executive at Trader Joe's, he had the opportunity to do so – to carve up and grow the company in ways that had never happened before. It was great training in retrospect, and a fantastic opportunity to not only build a national business but also an American brand that would be national in scope.

So at fifty-six years of age, after his initial retirement, Shields set out to be the CEO of the Trader Joe's chain. He would ultimately become the architect of its growth, elevating it to the national audience. When he first took control, he spent a lot of time reflecting on what the job entailed. As he looked at the company in its entirety, there were several things that were unique. One example was that there were only eight key people in a company that had six retail locations, and the only person that these eight key people had taken direction and orders from was Coulombe. Shields immediately thought that this structure was not prudent, especially since these eight people were all very upset that Coulombe was leaving the company and retiring.

Shields said all eight were terrified that with him taking over as CEO that they were in jeopardy of losing their jobs. Only one of the eight had a college degree.

"We were a little tiny company, and so the first morning, I got the eight of them together. We had a little tiny conference room. And I looked around the table, and I looked them in the eyes," Shield recalls. "I have always been sort of a gut type of person when I am dealing with people. By reading their eyes, I could tell that every one of those people thought that they were going to be fired that day. The first sentence that I said was that no one was being fired. I heard them all say, 'Phew.'"

However, Shields did say during that meeting with the managers that the company was going to undergo significant changes in the way it operated. He told them that from that point on, each one was fully responsible for every decision in the organization. "I know that this is going to come hard, because I know that you have not done this before, but I am going to help you, and I will train you and help guide you in making decisions in the process. The decision is going to be yours, and the responsibility is going to be yours," Shields remembers telling the eight terrified managers.

He went on to say that it would take two entire years for these eight managers to be comfortable in the role of being empowered to run their own stores. This type of macro change of management does not happen overnight. These managers had to realize that this speech was important and not sheer hot air, and they had to understand that Shields would stand by this management philosophy and back them up.

Trader Joe's in the Training Stages of Life—The SMART-U University

As Shields had mentioned earlier, he was extremely concerned about the overall lack of education throughout the organization, and he set out to correct that. In fact, most of the individuals who worked at Trader Joe's came straight out of high school with no college degree. For about two years, he found an executive who was at that time a CEO and chairman of a small group of stores that were based in Los Angeles. The executive had formerly been a professor at USC's graduate business school and had an association with a couple of ex-college professors who were running a little program that was called SMART-U. They had stopped teaching to focus on ways that would address the subject of business leadership. They all had lunch, and the men from SMART-U demonstrated their techniques of advancing business leadership and strategy. Shields immediately identified with their program and thought that it might be very helpful to use their services for training the employees at Trader Joe's. So Shields arranged an appointment for them to come to the corporate headquarters, visit their stores, and devise a possible strategy for training their employees. Shields was quite impressed with their plan, and as a result, they developed Trader Joe's SMART-U, short for SMART-U University.

"We developed Trader Joe's SMART-U, and it really was a series of building blocks in learning," Shields said. "But whatever they taught you in the morning, you could put to work that afternoon. Everything in this program was very practical. A lot of things were very simple, like saying thank you and all sorts of little things, and we have done that ever since."

So knowing that one of the first priorities for Shields was to implement the training and education program, he believed that the introduction of the Trader-Joe's SMART-U was an important first step in this process. As Shields led off with the campaign for training, he met with the eight managers to explain the training strategy. That same morning, Shields said he wanted each of them to take one page of paper and write a description of Trader Joe's Company. He wanted the managers to discuss what the company is all about and who the customers are that comprise their target market.

"Well, I got back eight pages, and none of them agreed," Shields said, laughing. "So, really the basis of my thoughts of leadership goes back to one thing: the leader has to have the vision of where he wants that organization to go. My gimmick is to take a yellow pad and draw a line down the middle. The left-hand side, I would say, 'Boy, if everything were perfect, what would this company look like?' On the right-hand side, I would say, 'What do we have to do to accomplish this?' It's very simple, but it works! Not only that, but this little exercise keeps you focused."

Trader Joe's in the Crawling Stages of Life—The Vision Plan Written

After about two years, Shields explains that he wrote the vision plan for the Trader Joe's Company. He said that he liked to keep his plan simple, and he was a great believer in simplicity in all aspects of business. His plan was comprised of the following sentences:

- We are going to be a chain of neighborhood, small, food stores.
- We will have unique products. We can't compete with Safeway or anybody like that, since we did not have that kind of money or capital.
- We can't sell Coke any cheaper than they could at Albertson's or Ralph's, so we must have products that would not be carried at these major grocery stores.
- By traveling the world, we, the product developers, would find new products and bring them back to the United States for consideration as a private label product under the Trader Joe's name. These products would give us a competitive advantage in this grocery business, which was notoriously low margin and low profit. The costs of traveling internationally would be part of the cost of doing business for Trader Joe's.

- We would adapt a friendly environment, with friendly and outgoing employees. This would create a happy environment and happy customers. The idea was that happy customers would spend more money in each store.
- We would dress in a Trader Joe's uniform, one that included short-sleeve Hawaiian printed shirts.

Trader Joe's in the Empowering the Leaders Stages of Life—More Power to the People

As Shields began to explain his vision for the company, which took him approximately two years to create, the importance of this first major step became very apparent as it also symbolized the future branding of the Trader Joe's that we now know and recognize. This was a huge first step for the growth of the company, and this strategy that was authored by John Shields was written over thirty-five years ago. It defined the evolution of a company with only six stores and seven hundred employees to a nationwide grocery store chain of over two hundred stores and thousands of employees!

The evolution of this strategy was largely dependent on several fronts, including defining the Trader Joe's brand, giving the management, the leaders of the company, the power to make decisions for their individual stores, and creating an environment where the company would grow with little debt on the balance sheet. Shields was a big believer that growth should be done carefully and cautiously. He also was a big believer that the private label for food and wine products would be an important part of their regional and national growth by catering to the needs of the customers on a local basis.

Shields gave the responsibility for the managers to be what he called product developers, instead of buyers. This enabled the small management team to research markets on an international basis through travel and find niche products that they believed would appeal to their local Trader Joe's stores. These products would then be brought back from overseas, tested in the marketplace of the stores and then rolled out as a private label product. You might find products in the Southern California area that would be quite different from the Northern California or Nevada regions. This increase in responsibility for the managers gave each of them a feeling of owning their individual Trader Joe's store and thus brought them a great deal of personal satisfaction from a standpoint of employment. They became very excited about what they were doing, and their motivation was greatly enhanced with this newfound responsibility, compared with their lack of motivation and empowerment when they worked directly under Joe Coulombe, the original founder. Shields said that these eight managers were so fulfilled by the work that each and every one of them continued to work as a leader until they retired.

Shields described his leadership philosophy and his desire to promote leaders from within the organization simply. "I would say that bringing in people from outside of the organization does not work that well. I would rather have the people who know and understand the business, and then I could teach them a lot," he said. "This is more like a teacher relationship. This is indeed part of empowering the people."

Trader Joe's in the Changing Stages of Life—From Small to Expansion

Shields knew that ultimately the company would start to grow slowly, and he knew that customers were generally very price sensitive. In the beginning, it was a slow evolution to grow the chain and to understand what customers wanted. His first inclination was to keep the company small and then build up to multiple locations. He knew that the private label food selection and the staff was a fundamental part of keeping the customers coming back to shop in their stores. The stores had to be staffed by friendly and fun people, and he did not mind if the employees were having fun while fulfilling their individual responsibilities. In fact, he believed that there would be greater sales and profits in a happy workplace.

Originally, Joe Coulombe had not wanted the stores to be within a fifteen-mile radius of each other. However, Shields decided to throw that philosophy out of the window, and soon there would be stores within one half of a mile apart, which seemed to work very well. Shields was very certain that he would start with slow and cautious growth and then lead to more and more stores throughout the western United States.

He had two driving factors for this philosophy: you retain your good people, and you attract good people. Shields saw this as natural for the expansion of the company. He also had several other positive and important factors that contributed to growth. Joe Coulombe had originally sold his company to a German family. They invested capital and did not want to take part in management of the company. It was a family trust, and he only saw them three days a year. They would come into the United States on the last Sunday of September. He would have them go through the stores. They had, and still have to this day, one of the largest chain stores in Europe. The German family also owns small grocery stores too. So Shields believes that is why they felt comfortable with buying Trader Joe's, since there were similarities to the businesses they were already managing. Shields even hypothesized that one of the main reasons that they were coming over to the United States was to get new ideas.

He told the owners about his strategy to grow the company, which would first come through analysis of the best regions to operate in. He continued by saying that the natural order would be to start in the areas that were closest to the original stores. That is when the company started expanding into Nevada and Arizona. At that particular time, they grew to approximately forty-five stores. Then the company further expanded into Oregon.

Trader Joe's—The Expansion into the Intelligent Communities of PhDs

Shields commented that since the company was privately owned and therefore had no board, he would often consult with his wife on business matters, who had a career in retail most of her life. He said that his wife became his advisor and an imaginary board member, and they would exchange ideas. In 1990, Shields became convinced that expansion beyond one hundred stores within three western United States would likely be unwise and oversaturated, and his wife and the owners agreed. They were already up to sixty-five stores in those three western states and would stop at one hundred.

He explained to the owners that if they were going to be a growth company, with locations in the hundreds, that they would need to develop into the Midwest and eastern United States. Shields believed that the best area to expand next would be the Chicago area, which was at that time the second largest food market in the United States.

Shields further explained his expansion strategy, and he mentioned that Coulombe had frequently spoken about the very intelligent population that was the customers of Trader Joe's. Shields said that Coulombe had believed in his gut that there were many unemployed PhDs that frequently shopped at their stores. This concept that they had discussed in years past raised interest in Shields as he continued to look for locations that they should be targeting for growth throughout the United States. Coincidentally, he found a magazine that showed the pockets of areas where highly educated individuals lived, which happened to be in areas that were situated around colleges and universities. One of the areas that the magazine article showed was located in a triangular region from Boston to New York City and Washington, DC. Before pursuing this new idea for further development, Shields decided that he would look at more research into this hypothesis of the "intelligent and well-educated" customers who were attracted to and shopped at Trader Joe's.

Shields discovered through his inquiries that the local graduate business school at UCLA had a team of business graduate students in that field of study. He explained that for only $2,500, you could have marketing research conducted on your business. Laughingly, he said that for that fee, you could have them do the whole research package, and obviously he felt that this was a fantastic opportunity to have UCLA do this research on Trader Joe's so that they could gain a new and better understanding of who their customer was and what the customers wanted. This would be typical of a marketing research project, and he felt that this money would be well worth the cost for this important information.

"They were charging $2,500 for the whole package. It was a terrific deal," he said. "I knew that we had a unique culture in the company, and how do you keep that core culture with core values to expand? That was a big issue; at least it was to me. We had plenty of money and no debt on our balance sheet, which was fantastic, and that is how I had envisioned the company's position at that point in time."

Shields asked the UCLA program to research company prospects on the East Coast of the United States, almost three thousand miles away. "I had the money to do it, I had the people, but can the culture go with us? They came back in about two months and said, 'Yes you can, but you are going to have to transfer about thirty people from California to wherever you want to go. That will allow you to keep your cadre, and they can build the company around them,' and we did."

Shields also asked the UCLA group to do another study interviewing customers. They developed a two-page questionnaire, and the professor said that Shields would be lucky to get a 3 percent response rate to the survey. So over a period from Thanksgiving to Christmas, the company sent out approximately two thousand surveys. To raise the number of respondents, Shields decided to put a two-dollar bill into each one of the surveys. "It was kind of unique because we had always been a wacky sort of company. The nature of the two-dollar bill made sense, and that quality is typical of Trader Joe's. We got a 78 percent response rate for the survey," Shields recalled.

Coulombe had predicted the market research showed that close to 80 percent of the Trader Joe's customers were pursuing a college degree, had already graduated from college, or had received graduate degrees.

Shields described how Coulombe had originally built Trader Joe's on two premises: one being to focus on educated customers. Before World War II, only 1 percent of the people in the United States had college degrees. Then the US Senate passed the GI Bill, and for the first time in the history of the country, more and more people graduated with college degrees. The second premise was the invention of the jet plane. Before the jet plane, only the very wealthy could afford to travel to Europe. With the rapid advancement of the jet plane, thus lowering the costs for air travel overseas, people with relatively modest means could go to Paris or London. So for the first time in the history of the United States, more people could experience the flavors of Europe. So Trader Joe's got to look at new foods and a whole series of things that were starting to happen. Coulombe told John Shields that if he could combine the ideas of education and travel, he would have a pretty neat company and those were the two founding principles of Trader Joe's.

Trader Joe's-Employees Shovel Snow in Their Hawaiian Short-Sleeve Shirts in Boston

The continuation of growth pushed toward Chicago and then onto the eastern United States, and the natural progression based on their market research was to place stores in the Boston area, with it being the educational capital of the country. With universities such as Harvard, Harvard Medical and Business School, University of Massachusetts, Boston College and Boston University, MIT, Tufts, amongst many others, it was an ideal place for Trader Joe's. At the time, Boston had about fifty universities within a fifty-mile radius. Shields boldly said, "Those are my customers for Trader Joe's!"

Soon Shields had the owners of Trader Joe's from Germany come and look at Boston as a new territory for growth of the chain. The owners had never seen Boston, and it was very apparent that they loved the community, since it had a very similar feeling to their homeland in Europe.

So they began to make their big jump into the northeastern area. Shields admitted that this was a very risky venture and he did not know of many retailers who had made this jump successfully. The model of the Trader Joe's chain was one based on many unique characteristics, such as the Hawaiian short-sleeve camp shirt and the khaki shorts. Obviously, this attire would be a real stretch in the subzero climate of Boston. Another risk in pursuing this new territory that was pointed out to Shields was that it would be highly unlikely to find the friendly, fun personnel that would be needed to continue in the ongoing strategy of Trader Joe's. Many told Shields he would not find those types of fun-loving people to work in the stores. With all of those naysayers, Shields said that he would be able to implement the dress code of the Hawaiian shirts in his stores and even laughed when he said that he had photographs of employees shoveling snow with their short-sleeve shirts and shorts.

Shields also believed he would have no problem finding friendly employees in Boston. He would visit local restaurants and look for the waiters and waitresses who were fun and passionate about serving their customers. He explained that these individuals would be the pool of employees that he would talk to and later have his staff interview for jobs at the local Trader Joe's locations. This implementation of seeking out new employees proved to be very successful for the company. For those friendly individuals who were hired, they would soon be put through the SMART-U program. They were trained and educated for one year, and within one year they were considered to be Trader Joe's employees. Apparently the system worked like a charm, but as Shields explained, you have to train them each and every day. However, Shields is adamant that if you have a bad employee, you have to get rid of them. It is critical to get those bad employees out of the pool.

Trader Joe's—The Power of the Private Label

Shields further explained that the research costs related to European private label foods and spirits greatly enhanced the sales and profits of the company, since these products were not readily available at other stores. And with the increased European travel, Americans had an enhanced appetite for European food products, which Trader Joe's was able to provide. Shields explained that the products would be flown in from Europe, and there would be market testing done for each product. Based on the outcome of these surveys, and often different communities would provide different foods based on the needs of the local community, they would be implemented into the Trader Joe's system. He said the managers of each store would make their own recommendations. Shields called these managers the "ship captains," who would steer the store toward certain products, thus further empowering their leadership. If the international products successfully passed the tests of popularity, then the local subcontractors would make the foods and process them. This job of manufacturing the food and the spirits was strictly the job of the subcontractors. Trader Joe's did not take part in this manufacturing process, and Shields said that throughout the decades Trader Joe's has been in business, many of these subcontractors became multimillionaires.

"Yes, and we do not make anything ourselves, but we have a lot of people here in Los Angeles, even on the East Coast now, who can make our products for us," Shields said. "They are usually very small businesses, and we have made a lot of millionaires out of these subcontractors over the years. They are happy, and we are very happy."

If you ask Shields about the success of the chardonnay wine, the Two Buck Chuck, he'll credit them with propelling the company's wine business into becoming a major source of revenue. He also mentioned that the plant and orchid business had become another very important category for Trader Joe's, and they worked with local growers throughout the country to expand the growing plant and the cut-flower business.

Trader Joe's—The Power of the Small Size

Shields went onto describe several other factors that were important in the growth of the company, such as the often small size of the retail locations. He mentioned that he liked the size of the store being small, with multiple checkout stands so people can shop and check out as quickly as possible. Or as he described it, "Get in and out very fast." He said that with a larger store, such efficiency would not be possible. Shields also said that the rent paid for the Trader Joe's stores is extremely cheap. In addition, the company's advertising is largely word of mouth, keeping advertising expenses extremely low.

Laughingly, he also described that the parking lot size was small, since as they first started to increase the number of stores, they underestimated the demand and the numbers of customers that would shop at Trader Joe's. "What happened is that we had much more business than we had originally thought that we would have," he said.

Trader Joe's—Boots on the Ground—The People Thing!

As Shields reflects back on his career at Trader Joe's and the profound impact that he had as being the primary architect of building the brand and growing the stores from six locations to several hundred, he began to describe several more key strategic objectives for success.

He spoke of the importance of reaching out on a personal basis to the customers, employees, and management of Trader Joe's. Shield's normal schedule would be to visit multiple stores per week and talk to everybody in the store, and he did not care if the employee had only recently been hired or if it was a management-level employee. This "boots on the ground" mentality was a very crucial element in understanding the human connection, Shields said, leading to a greater understanding of the day-to-day needs for management. He felt that it was fundamentally important to be in touch with the people, or as he called it "the people thing."

"I made a rule to myself that I had to spend two full days in Trader Joe's stores per week. I have never believed that you should run a company from your desk," he said. "I could do, depending on the distance, three to four stores per day. I would just ask them where they went to school and how they were doing."

Shields said that when an employee would respond that they were just okay, he would stop and ask what was wrong, furthering his connection to the team. "We also have a very low employee turnover rate, which is less than 1 percent. And that is tremendously important to the success of an organization, and therefore lowering costs of training employees, etc." He stated that his employees are very highly paid, and these wages are well worth it. At the time of the interview, Trader Joe's had approximately 40,000 employees.

The Albrecht family is the owner of the company. The family also owns the ALDI Grocery chain of stores, which adds up to some eight thousand locations. Nonetheless, the family was very hands-off in managing Trader Joe's, allowing Shields to lead the company. He also added that they never took any dividends out of the company but always reinvested it into the chain. Shields explained that that was one of the reasons that he decided against franchising the business, acquiring other companies, and making the very important decision to stay an American brand. Shields believed that it would be better to grow the chain on a national basis with eight hundred stores than to go international. He mentioned that they currently have about four hundred stores and are progressing toward doubling the size of their chain. Shields said the grocery chain has very impressive annual sales on a company-wide basis, which is truly a remarkable feat for a company that started with six stores when John Shields took over as chief executive.

Trader Joe's—The Importance of Creating Customer Value and Loyalty

Shields further believes in the importance of creating and constantly expanding the value of the chain for the customer. It is critically important that you know as a customer when you go to Trader Joe's that you are going to consistently have a number of things.

- friendly service
- great products
- great prices
- access to items that can't be found anywhere else

Shields's story reminds one of the most recent stories in financial news, which details the direct competition between Trader Joe's and Whole Foods. Trader Joe's is beating Whole Foods in profit margins and is also taking away market share from the grocer. But with all of this tremendous success and the wealth that comes with it, Shields would still go back to work in a heartbeat.

"Oh I would go back to work tomorrow, if I could. I just thought to myself that since I didn't need the money, I will retire. So that is what I did. I retired after being chief executive officer of Trader Joe's for thirty years. My experience at Macy's and Mervyn's gave me a tremendous amount of experience in retail. In both instances, I was the VP of operations and gained a lot of insight into retail in these stores.

"Anyway, it was a great ride, and I loved every minute of it. Speaking of rides, I need to go over to my friend's house next door, Steve Dorfman, to ask him about an issue that I am having with my television signal! I am sure that you would be fascinated with his career as vice chairman of Hughes Electronics Corporation and chairman of Hughes Telecommunications and Space Corporation!"

The following two exhibits on leadership and characteristics of companies with great strength were personally provided for this chapter by Mr. John Shields:

Leadership—In the Eyes of John Shields

"First, the terms CEO and leader are not synonymous. CEOs are measured by sales, profits, etc. Leaders are shaped by and defined by character. Leaders inspire and enable others to do outstanding work and realize their potential. Leaders build success and enduring organizations. True leaders are ethical. They believe in what is the right thing to do—not what is legal.

"Leaders confer responsibility and authority on their people.

"Leaders allow their people to make mistakes and learn from them.

"A leader is a coach, not a dictator.

"Leaders articulate a clear vision of the goal.

"Leaders articulate this specific, consistent vision to their people and enable their people to share this vision. They sell the benefits of achieving this vision.

"Leaders are optimistic.

"Leaders get out of the office and listen to their people and customers.

"Leaders know their customers.

"Leaders keep focused.

"Leaders give their people the tools that they need and get out of their way.

"Leaders share the company's success with their people.

"Leaders are not afraid to take reasonable risks.

"Leaders have a passion that inspires others.

"Leaders have courage and stick to their beliefs. They are able to survive setbacks, heartbreaks and learn from them.

"Leaders have judgment, which results from asking questions of really wise people.

"Leaders understand and practice WIN—what's important now. They prioritize.

"Leaders know how to allocate their time and energy.

"Leaders have an innate sense of humor.
"Leaders encourage experimentation.
"Leaders develop other leaders—not managers."

Characteristics of a Strong Company, as Told by John Shields

1. A simple business model. Easily understood by management, employees, and customers. Focused. Easy to see how it makes money.
2. A wide moat advantage: differentiation in the market.
3. Repeated cash flow.
4. Low inventory risk. Fast turn—no markdowns.
5. Alignment of Interests. Clear goals shared by management and employees.
6. A healthy culture. People feel that they are a part of a visionary, honest, ethical, and loyal team.
7. A flat organizational structure. High revenues per person.
8. Low capital requirements. Company doesn't need a lot of cash.
9. Low reinvention risk. A product line that does not have to be changed every year. Food.
10. Resilient demographic / industrial positioning. Ability to recognize trends and act on them.

In investing, each company must be measured in context, considering its industry, regulatory environment, demographics, and price.

Chapter 3

Steve Dorfman, Hughes Space and Communications-Former CEO, Contributed to Cable and Direct TV
The Scientist Who Helped Changed the World
A True Pioneer in the Cable Industry and Space Technology

Steve Dorfman

Imagine an age when technology as we know it today simply did not exist. It was a world with no cell phones, let alone smartphones, no satellites, no global communication, no weather satellite technology, and no cable television networks. The television industry had three channels from which to choose, and those channels were only available to view in black and white.

Now fast-forward to a fight of epic proportions, which was seen around the world through HBO, the fight known as the "Thrilla in Manila." The historic bout between Muhammad Ali and Joe Frazier on October 1, 1975, went fifteen nail-biting rounds, rising to be one of the greatest and most memorable boxing matches of all time.

The "Thrilla in Manila" Fight Served as a Catalyst for Satellite Communications

"Of all the men I fought, Sonny Liston was the scariest, George Foreman was the most powerful, Floyd Patterson was the most skilled as a boxer," Ali once said. "But the roughest and toughest was Joe Frazier. He brought out the best in me, and the best fight we fought was in Manila." Frazier had won their first fight, and Ali the second. It was 10:45 a.m. in the Philippines when they got underway, though the entire world, including Steve Dorfman, was watching.

When the bell rang for the fifteenth round, Frazier, with his eyes almost completely shut, remained in his corner as his trainer, Eddie Futch, threw in the towel. "Man, I hit him with punches that'd bring down the walls of a city," Frazier said. "Lawdy, lawdy, he's a great champion!" Ali had fought his way to become the heavyweight champion of the world in one of the most important fights in history.

As millions of people from all over the planet were watching, Dorfman and the scientists at Hughes, one of the largest satellite manufacturers in the world, were watching with keen interest. At the time, Hughes happened to be the largest employer in the state of California. Hughes led the world in satellite communication technology. This technology was pioneered by the brilliant Hughes, Cal Tech engineer, Harold Rosen with the launch of Syncom in 1963. The scientists and executives of Hughes saw huge potential as the broadcast was televised successfully via four Hughes-built satellites owned by Intelsat to all parts of the world, and then by the RCA Company to HBO in the United States. This major television event was the brainchild of an individual by the name of Jerry Levin, an executive at HBO / Time Warner. Prior to this boxing match, HBO started out as a small distributor in the New York area and was owned by Time Warner. With the huge success of this fight, Jerry Levin would soon be catapulted into superstardom at HBO / Time Warner.

Dorfman remembers how the event would serve as motivation and inspiration for a business he would lead at Hughes for years to come. "Time Incorporated had formed a new business unit called HBO to provide additional pay services, featuring sports and movies," he said. "This business was struggling when Jerry Levin had the idea of distributing the HBO TV service over satellites to cable operators throughout the country. HBO leased two transponders on the RCA Satcom, a competitor of Hughes Communications, and on September 30, 1975, the famous boxing match was televised, and it helped launch HBO into a profitable business, which soon expanded rapidly with the business model of distributing their programing through satellites."

As Dorfman watched the event via television, he could envision the revolution of cable television in its infancy being launched before his eyes. This is the man who so elegantly married science and technology with commerce to create great profit. This man would ultimately become the chief executive of Hughes Communications.

Breaking the Satellite Mold and Thinking outside of the Boxing Ring

Dorfman and his Hughes Communications team were responsible for taking this breakthrough technology of cable television and adding value. By 1983, he and his team at Hughes Communications were able to take much of the market share away from RCA.

"RCA made a number of errors, and one of them was providing service on a common carrier basis, where everybody paid the same nondiscriminatory rate," Dorfman said. At the time, HBO was looking for another company to work with besides RCA, and through due diligence, they chose Hughes Communications. Their decision to diversify was reinforced when a replacement RCA satellite failed to reach orbit. "We were fortunate that the cable industry was seeking alternates to RCA, and they became interested in our first commercial satellite, Galaxy I, which became dedicated to the cable industry. Instead of leasing at tariff rates like our competitors, we were able to sell transponders and obtain cash for building Galaxy II and III. We sold our first six transponders to HBO at favorable rates, and they became our anchor tenant, in much the same way a quality department store becomes the anchor tenant for a shopping mall."

To induce cable operators to point their antennas at Hughes's Galaxy satellite, the company gave away free antennas to all cable operators, making its orbital slot prime property. Soon, the many cable programmers were competing against each other to get their transponders on the Hughes satellites. And this business model became a huge profit creator for Hughes. For a transponder that was sold for up to $14 million, it only cost Hughes $3 million to produce. This radical idea of selling the transponders instead of selling the entire satellite and creating a desirable satellite location was a breakthrough business decision made by the Hughes Communications team.

The business environment for building and selling satellites for Hughes and their competitors prior to the 1975 boxing fight was becoming increasingly oversaturated with production and inventory. With this competitive market, the profit was becoming more and more marginal as well. The typical markup at Hughes satellite would be in the single digits. Furthermore, the business risks of delivering complicated satellites on fixed-price contracts were high. Therefore, even though Hughes had a major market share in the satellite field, with the advent of other competitors from the United States and Europe, the business began to shrink, and contracts became increasingly difficult to obtain.

Dorfman and his colleagues saw the huge potential in this new industry. They would reframe the old business model at Hughes of selling satellites to selling the transponders to the cable programmers, and instead of a 9 percent markup, the company could receive a 450 percent markup. By selling the total package, they would break the satellite into pieces, giving them about twenty-four transponders to sell, which resulted in sales exceeding $200 million per satellite launched. And this was partially a result of giving away free antennas to all cable operators, thus largely undermining the competition, such as RCA. This radical new business idea, which Dorfman called "going up the value chain," gave Hughes a tremendous competitive advantage. Dorfman also mentioned that Hughes Communications was the only company that was using this model at the time; however, years later, other companies would copy their business model. For those that may not fully understand what a transponder is, it is what gathers signals over a range of uplink frequencies and retransmits them on a different set of downlink frequencies to receivers to Earth, without changing the content of the received signal or signals. The connections between the galaxy satellite system and the cable industry was as Dorfman called it, "definitely a symbiotic relationship," which enabled the cable industry to grow while enabling the Hughes satellite technology to become the most profitable segment in the very diversified and complex corporation of Hughes. This gained Dorfman greater status as an important turnaround leader who could lead the industry into the future. In fact, Dorfman had previously been head of the Venus exploration segment of Hughes, which was another example of the symbiotic relationship between space and communications.

Dorfman Adds More Prestigious Clients to the Hughes Rolodex

The opportunities of satellite distribution of cable programing caught the attention of not only Dorfman and the Hughes Communications executives but also none other than the "Mouth of the South" and "Captain Outrageous"—Ted Turner. A southern man from Atlanta, Turner graduated from the Georgia Military Academy and later came back home to take over his father's advertising agency, Turner Advertising. He became president and chief executive in 1963. By 1970, Turner had grown his advertising firm into the biggest in the Southeastern United States and eventually purchased several radio and television stations.

Ted Turner had a similar vision, thinking he could take this technology of cable satellites and marry it with his Turner Broadcasting Company. This would turn a small local cable distributor into an international powerhouse, an idea that would make him one of the wealthiest men in America. In 1976, Turner decided to go forward with this business decision to integrate cable satellites with his fledging business, TBS.

Turner was looking to purchase much-needed transponders from Hughes to launch his cable station, based in Atlanta, to be called the Turner Broadcasting Company or TBS. Turner knew that Hughes was the only game in town, and that gave him few options to negotiate pricing for these transponders. He soon found out that there were very few other alternatives for competitive pricing in the niche industry, and soon, Turner would be going into a buzz saw.

"Ted Turner is quite a character, and I got to know him reasonably well," Dorfman said. "I did quite a lot of business with him, providing satellite communications for his Turner Broadcasting Company. Also, Hughes Communications would be providing satellite services for his newly formed Cable News Network or CNN." The fledging 24/7 news network was launched in 1980.

In the 1980s, Turner also purchased the library of Metro-Goldwyn-Mayer, better known as MGM, with such well-known movies as *Gone with the Wind* and *The Wizard of Oz*. The decision to purchase such a large and historical film library was a very lucrative decision for the Turner Broadcasting Company.

Dorfman said Turner became tough to negotiate with as he felt pricing at Hughes was too high. "He once said he would never pay such a high price for another transponder from Hughes," Dorfman recalled. Turner ended up being the largest worldwide buyer of transponders and owed a huge amount of his accumulated wealth from the sale in 1996 of Turner Broadcasting to Time Warner for $7.5 billion. This information is also relevant today as we read about several mergers and acquisitions, such as the possible purchase of Time Warner by Fox for close to $80 billion and Direct TV to be purchased by AT&T for $48.5 billion.

Satellite Distribution of HBO, TBS, CNN Was Critical for the Development of Hughes Communications

Dorfman continued by saying the profits that funneled into the Hughes business were a critical element to the health of the overall Hughes Aircraft Company. "We did quite well with our first several satellites named Galaxy I, II, and III," he said. "At one point in time, the small Hughes Communications, called a subsidiary at the time, became the most profitable unit in the company primarily because we were doing so well with our customers in the cable industry." Dorfman became a pioneer in the communications industry, and he mentioned that, "Part of my job was to convert the technology to profits." What Dorfman really did was help bring cable to the world.

The Evolution of Direct TV and the Fight against Cannibalization

Dorfman remained forward thinking.

"After all of this success, we took a deep breath and asked where would we go next, and what kind of future might we build? In the early eighties, we saw three new applications of satellites that would be very useful:

- satellite transmission of TV direct to homes;
- mobile communications using satellites; and
- telecommunication networking using small dishes and satellites.

We eventually converted all three applications into businesses, which continue to this day."

At that point in time, dishes for cable TV distribution were six to twelve feet in dimension; few people owned their own dishes capable of receiving TV. One year in a Neiman-Marcus Christmas catalogue, which always had the gift of the year, there was the suggestion to buy your loved one a six-foot satellite dish for $10,000 or so. Dorfman exclaimed that he believed at the time that this was truly the "Gift of the Year."

"So people were intercepting the cable distribution with big dishes, but what we saw was the possibility of more powerful satellites and smaller dishes and what ultimately became Direct TV, but it took us a while to get there, a long while," he said. "And so the FCC was putting out an opening for companies to apply for the direct broadcast frequencies; the allocations of frequencies in the geostationary orbit is very critical. At that point in time, people didn't really understand how critical it was, but we did. And so we applied for direct broadcast satellite frequencies. We also applied for mobile satellite communications.

"This was in 1984, and previously I have discussed mistakes that RCA made in their overall business strategy in relation to satellite communications. RCA had their direct broadcast frequencies, and surprisingly, they gave them up." He said the group had some very farsighted people there at the working level that thought that direct-to-home broadcasting would be useful, but the company elected to surrender their frequencies. In 1984, Hughes got its frequencies, and Dorfman worked with his team to push forward with new technologies for these dishes. It took ten years to resolve all the technical and programming issues, but during those ten years, the technology evolved to make direct-to-home TV even more powerful, and Dorfman said the company was very fortunate. "Years later, people were bidding half a billion dollars for these frequencies that we got for free," Dorfman said.

Dorfman said the first thing that they found was obtaining the necessary TV programming was extremely challenging, and there was a very simple reason for it. There were a lot of people and lobbyists that were against direct-to-home TV because it bypassed a lot of infrastructure and just focused on one part of the cable industry. "To give an example, take one of our major cable industry customers, Time Warner. There are two parts of the cable industry; one is the programming part, and the other is the operational companies, such as the distributors or cable companies," he said. "With the Time Warner Company, having an HBO division tied into their company, you had the following dynamic, which made the development of Direct TV very difficult. You had Time Warner investing billions of dollars in infrastructure, digging holes and running cable." Dorfman said Time Warner and their lobbyists did not by any means want to accept the idea of taking their company away from the cable industry model. In other words, a Direct TV dish that could be purchased directly for each home would take out Time Warner's subscription base from their customers. On the other hand, within Time Warner, you had HBO saying and lobbying in favor of the direct-to-home technology. HBO said, "Yes, we are on board with this Direct TV idea."

"We are going to make this happen, and we will work with you, Hughes Communications," Dorfman said. "Time Warner said absolutely not, and if you do proceed with this new technology, it will destroy our business, and it will cannibalize not only our business but the industry." This tension existed for a number of years and stopped Hughes from moving forward with this new technology of direct-to-home TV. Imagine two competing strategies from within one company, Time Warner, and its segment of HBO. It was quite a puzzle that took years for Dorfman at Hughes Communications to solve.

"So that's where it stayed for a number of years, and we just couldn't get the combination going, and we ourselves were conflicted, because our major customer were the programmers, and we were caught in the middle," he said. "I remember once in a meeting with Viacom's executive who said, 'We will go along with you if you indemnify us for all the business that we are going to lose with the cable industry,' because the cable operators had the threat of not carrying the programming."

Cable Act of 1980, Led by Al Gore, and the Link to Direct TV

"This stall continued until, I know this is going to be a startling statement, until Al Gore stepped in," Dorfman recalled. The reason was based on the Cable Act of 1980. Al Gore was working on a cable bill to try to put a brake on the growth of cable prices that were offending people. "And as he was part of putting together the Cable Act Bill, he injected into the bill a clause which said that all sources of communications must carry the programming," Dorfman said. "In other words, you can't turn down the programming once offered. And that broke the deadlock."

Dorfman said the programmers were captive to the operators because the operators were threatening that if they went someplace else, they would be denied access to the cable business, and that would kill them. HBO could be out of business in a year if they couldn't get access to the cable systems. "But now HBO could say it must provide programming to alternate sources, which was us, DirecTV, and that really opened up the possibility of proceeding with what became DirecTV, which required the frequencies which we had; required the high-power satellite, which we developed," he said. "It required financing, which was permitted because we started lining up the programs, including HBO and the others. And with that, we proceeded with direct-to-home."

There was also another thing about the timing that was important. It is a technical detail, but it was an important detail, which is the development of solid-state devices that were inexpensive, exemplified by Moore's law. He also gives the general parameters to Moore's law, which was first recognized by the cofounder of Intel, Gordon Moore, in which he described that the number of transistors per square inch on integrated circuits had doubled every two years since their invention, thus lowering costs of encryption and decryption. And what that did is permit digitizing the signals. It permitted low-cost receivers. It permitted low-cost encryption and decryption. "And all of a sudden, we had a system that was much more powerful than the one we started with ten years ago, which was an analog system," Dorfman said.

It became apparent to Dorfman that with the push into direct-to-home TV technology, more sophisticated and powerful satellites were needed. This would enable homeowners to own smaller and less expensive satellite dishes. At this time, Hughes was soon to be sold to General Motors due to the nature of the complexity of the will of the late founder, Howard Hughes. The bulk of the will endowed the Howard Hughes Medical Institute with the Hughes Aircraft Company. After the death of Howard Hughes, it was thought by the trustees that it would be best to divest all or part of Hughes Aircraft Company. Many competing bids were considered, such as Ford, Boeing, and General Motors, who were also interested in purchasing the company. This would allow the Howard Hughes Medical Institute to be less dependent on one asset, the Hughes Aircraft Company. Ultimately, General Motors won the bid to purchase the Hughes Company.

"Along the line with our direct-to-home strategy, we decided we needed more powerful satellites, and it required an investment of about $100 million to develop a new satellite system to be higher power for all applications, but in my mind especially direct-to-home," Dorfman said. "The more powerful the satellite, the smaller the dish, and we wanted these dishes to be small for the public to be able to afford. So asking for a $100 million investment shortly after the sale of Hughes to General Motors, we knew would be a tremendous challenge."

Nonetheless, Dorfman and his colleagues went to GM in Detroit and spoke to the vice chairman, Don Atwood, spending about ten minutes describing their plan. Don Atwood, without hesitation, gave Hughes his blessing, enabling the company to develop a new generation of satellites with higher power. Dorfman said that originally he was very concerned about the sale of Hughes to General Motors; however, he ultimately discovered that their management style was very hands-off and left most of the strategy to the executives at Hughes. He said that GM did not try to manage their business, a decision reinforced by the continued growth and success of the Hughes team.

"So again, the timing was right. It took a period of ten years to enable this technology of DirecTV to be developed," he said. "To give you an overview of the structure of this Hughes division, it was structured accordingly: DirecTV was part of Hughes Communications, and Hughes Communications was part of the Hughes Space and Communications Group, and the Space and Communications group was part of Hughes Aircraft Company. Hughes had mastered the capability of forming entrepreneurial groups within a large corporation. I offer Eddy Hartenstein as an example of the quality of people I worked with at Hughes and the entrepreneurial spirit that we built up at Hughes Communications. Eddy, a Cal Tech graduate, was part of the system engineering team for the Venus exploration project that I managed in the late 1970s. Eddy later joined Hughes Communications where he helped us make the Galaxy Program a major success. He subsequently took over our direct-to-home TV business, named it DirecTV, and brought the business to fruition with its launch in 1994. He stayed on as a leader of that business until Rupert Murdoch purchased the business. After leaving Hughes, he became the CEO of the *Los Angeles Times*.

"Another example was Tom Whitehead, a PhD from MIT who was hired by Bud Wheelon as an advisor after Tom had led the move to deregulate telecommunications as a member of the Nixon administration. Tom advised Bud to start up Hughes Communication to take advantage of the deregulation, which he understood so well, and Bud asked Tom to be the first CEO, and he asked me to be Tom's principal deputy. Tom formulated some of the original strategies that I have discussed, but he soon left Hughes, and I took over as CEO. It was my privilege to work with these individuals and many others who contributed to my success and the success of Hughes.

"Ultimately, the Hughes Aircraft Company disappeared as a company. General Motors eventually decided to sell off Hughes, which they did at a significant profit." Dorfman went on to explain that they originally paid about $5 billion for Hughes, and they probably made $20 billion or more selling off the pieces. "So it was probably one of the best investments that GM had ever made," he said. Dorfman further described how Hughes got sold off by segments. "The defense part of our business was sold to Raytheon, the satellite manufacturing business was sold to Boeing, and the DirecTV business was sold to Rupert Murdoch, and so on."

"Now, I have got to get back to me, because during this time period, Bud Wheelon, who was head of the Space and Communications Group, was promoted to run the entire company. I was asked to move from running Hughes Communications, which had been very successful, to go to our parent, which was the Space and Communications Group," Dorfman said. So now you can see this kind of a hierarchy—Space and Communications Group, Hughes Communications, which was the son of the Space and Communications Group, and then DirecTV, which was the son of Hughes Communications. Dorfman became the number-two guy and then ultimately became CEO of the entire Space and Communications Group in the 1990s and then the vice chairman of Hughes. Dorfman retired in 1999. "I felt that I had a successful career at Hughes; however, it was time to move on."

Dorfman goes on to reflect on the final stages of the Hughes Company and how the major units were acquired by other corporations. DirecTV was purchased by AT&T for $50 billion. Boeing purchased the Satellite Manufacturing unit and the Space and Communications Group. Raytheon purchased the defense portion of Hughes. The Hughes Communication unit continues under that name as part of the Equatorial Corporation. Dorfman said that these companies that came out of Hughes continue to be productive units carrying on the high technology and entrepreneurial tradition of Hughes.

One could conclude that after the multiple breakup and sale of the Hughes conglomerate and the sale of their units had reached a conclusion, this was the final and ending stage of the Hughes organization. This was staggering since the Hughes conglomerate had, at a point in time, been the biggest employer of the state of California. The end of the Hughes Company was also astonishing as one considers the sheer amount of innovation that was created by the very entrepreneurial Hughes organization. Symbolically, the end of the Hughes organization was much like a shining, brilliant comet, leaving millions of bits of information and technology in its wake, and ultimately, Hughes would come to a fateful ending.

However, that would not be the case, as Dorfman goes onto explain the far-reaching and lasting legacy of Hughes. Dorfman suggests, "The most lasting and important legacy of Hughes is the Howard Hughes Medical Institute (HHMI), which sold Hughes to General Motors in 1983 but continued to own appreciating Hughes stock." The value of the work of the many scientists and engineers like Dorfman is represented by the current Howard Hughes Medical Institute (HHMI) endowment, which has appreciated to $19 billion. This supports about $700 million a year in medical research, supporting 2,500 people involved in biomedical research. Twenty-five individuals have been awarded Nobel Laureates as a result of their work in this medical institute. This, Dorfman says, "is the most satisfying legacy of his Hughes career."

The Breadth of Steve Dorfman's Accomplishments

The story of how Dorfman was able to accomplish such a feat is the tale of a man who was accomplished on multiple levels and achieved remarkable things in his life. His foundation was rooted in the science of electro-optics, radar, infrared technology, planetary space exploration, weather satellites, and breakthrough technologies. Perhaps his greatest contribution, however, was his ability to merge innovation and creativity, which led to hundreds of new technologies that we continue to be influenced by today.

The names of the companies that Dorfman was associated with read like a who's who in these fields of technology. He received NASA's most prestigious award as NASA's Distinguished Public Service Medal in 1979; he was catapulted to the vice chairman position of Hughes Electronics Corporation, which had annual sales of $10 billion in 1999; and was also chair of Hughes Telecommunication and Space Company. Dorfman was one of the most effective leaders in the infancy of space telecommunications and planetary exploration. He and his teams launched the industry of telecommunications as we know it today. These businesses either did not exist or were in their infant stages. Dorfman played a key role in developing these businesses, such as cable capabilities for HBO, Time Warner, Turner

Broadcasting Service, CNN-Cable News Network, and DirecTV and others. Dorfman was also a key strategist for the innovation of electro-optics, weather satellites, and exploratory missions to Venus and Jupiter. The Venus explorations would enable the testing of the greenhouse effects on the planet, and those results could be used to correlate the similarities of the greenhouse effect here on our planet, Earth. This robotic research was done decades in advance of greenhouse gases becoming a household term.

As one begins to contemplate the breadth of the accomplishments of Steve Dorfman at Hughes, it is a very daunting task to dissimilate the information, the history, and the chronology of these events and of his career path. But it's impossible to understand this path that he took in his life and in his career choices without first looking at his young adult life in school. Only then can you follow the ideas that propelled him into a leadership role at Hughes.

The Ideas That Propelled Steve Dorfman from a Student into Space Technology

The Catalyst for Dorfman—The Sputnik Launch in 1957

One can only imagine the path that Steve Dorfman took to begin his education as a young adult, eventually becoming the successful scientific executive that he became. Dorfman began by saying that there was certainly a spark that set him toward a mission to pursue science and space technology. "I believe that I was fortunate in timing. The year was 1957, and I graduated in the year that Russia launched the Sputnik rocket. The launch of the Russian Sputnik satellite led to the escalation of the Cold War with Russia, thus propelling the United States into the creation of their space program."

As it is described in the NASA website, "History changed on October 4, 1957, when the Soviet Union successfully launched Sputnik I. The world's first artificial satellite was about the size of a beach ball (58 cm. or 22.8 inches in diameter), weighed only 83.6 kg. or 183.9 pounds, and took about 98 minutes to orbit the Earth on its elliptical path. That launch ushered in new political, military, technological, and scientific developments. While the Sputnik launch was a single event, it marked the start of the space age and the U.S. vs. U.S.S.R-Russia space race."

Dorfman continues to describe this singular event that had such a powerful effect on his future, since he could envision becoming an integral part of this space race for exploration between the two superpowers. This event would trigger his imagination both academically and intellectually. As Dorfman describes, in 1957 after he graduated from the University of Florida, he received a Hughes Fellowship for a master's program at USC (University of Southern California.) He successfully completed his master's program and soon became immersed in the field of electro-optics and became part of a team working to design systems to shoot down Soviet bombers and missiles. This team was ultimately merged into a newly formed space division of Hughes. Dorfman said, "I was surrounded and fell in with a bunch of very smart people. So I had a lot of good luck to get where I got. I do not want to minimize seizing the opportunities and hard work, I did all of those things, but it was within a framework of good fortune in terms of timing, in terms of the people that I got associated with."

The Importance of Working as a Team at Hughes—And Giving More Than You Are Asked to Do for Your Bosses

He commented, "He would say that you do whatever your boss asks you to do and do it well, and you are sure to get more and more responsibility, which is what I did. Make sure that you have good bosses, since there is a correlation here!"

So Dorfman got involved and engaged in space first by demonstrating his gift for understanding infrared technology, which led to him being involved in some of the highly classified programs in the defense department of Hughes Aircraft. Dorfman was ultimately moved to a job where he was responsible for developing new programs in the civil space area.

Bud Wheelon, formerly the CIA deputy director of the research and development, became head of the newly formed Hughes Space and Communications Group. Bud Wheelon successfully accomplished a major reorganization strategy at Hughes by dividing Hughes into three core divisions: 1) Defense-Military, which was classified programs, 2) Commercial Communications, and 3) NASA Division.

Dorfman's Accomplishments at Hughes

Dorfman helped to introduce the weather satellite, the Earth Resources Sensor, and the Venus Probe, and he was awarded NASA's highest civilian honor—the Distinguished Public Service Medal.

    At the beginning of his career at Hughes, Dorfman was given the assignment of working with the NASA Division to develop new businesses with NASA. Dorfman explains, "I was quite good at it, as a matter of fact, developing a track record of winning new business. Using my background in electro-optics, I was able to lead in the development of a multispectral scanner for sensing agriculture crops from space. This type of device, pioneered by Hughes, is still used to this day. I also led the development of monitoring weather from geostationary orbit and sold the first geostationary meteorological satellite to the Japanese government. Later we sold a similar system called the geostationary operational environmental satellite to NASA. Both of these satellite systems evolved over many decades and continue to be used today and are vital for weather forecasting and for predicting crop health. My string of new business successes continued with my leading an effort to win a major contract from the NASA Ames Research Center to build two spacecrafts to orbit Venus and land four probes on the surface. The valuation of this contract would be close to $300 million in today's dollars. These probes would enable our atmospheric scientists to learn more about a comparable planet, Venus, in our solar system and the impact that the greenhouse effect had on Venus, as it might be similar to the greenhouse effect on Earth. This time, my bosses asked me to manage the full project despite my relatively young age and inexperience. At first, I declined, but I was overruled by my boss. NASA wanted me to oversee the project. It turned out to be a good outcome for me since I had the satisfaction of managing the program to a successful rendezvous and landing on Venus in 1978. For my efforts, I was awarded the NASA Distinguished Public Service Medal. This medal was the highest honor for civilians. I then became the head of the

Hughes NASA Division, and we continued building weather satellites and planetary exploration spacecraft for Venus and Jupiter. It was a fun time for me, and I was rewarded by being inducted in the National Academy of Engineering, the most distinguished status an engineer can achieve."

Dorfman continued, "Then one day, Bud Wheelon called me asking that I join a new Hughes startup, Hughes Communication. This was a new business for me, and I had to work seven days a week to catch up to this new business environment. I soon became head of this small company, which, as I described earlier, changed Hughes Aircraft forever. After Bud was promoted to run all of Hughes Aircraft, I was moved back to the Space and Communications Group, where I ultimately became head of that operation.

"On my wall is the NASA Distinguished Public Service Medal, which I won for running that program, which is the highest award that NASA gives. This now takes us back to me moving from the NASA side of Hughes to the Hughes Communications side, which we previously discussed. I will say that during my lifetime, this has been a tremendously exciting ride through space, exploration, and communications, and I have added a list of ideas that I believe are very critical to becoming a successful business leader. Thank you once again for listening to my story, and hopefully you will benefit from my life's experience."

Steve Dorfman's Key Principles for Business Leadership

Steve Dorfman reflected on what made him successful and offered up some thoughts that might be generally useful.

Make Your Own Luck: "I was fortunate to join a great group at Hughes, but I had many opportunities when I graduated college and selected Hughes to be the most promising."

Seize the Opportunities: "I lived in a time of rapidly evolving technology, which persists to this day, and I found those opportunities that seemed most promising to me and pursued them aggressively and persistently. They were not all successful, but my batting average was good."

Do What Is Asked of You and Do It Well: "I worked within an organization and found if I did what my boss asked and did it well, I got increased responsibilities and rewards. I strove to find good bosses."

Create a Great Team: "I found that as I got more responsibility that it was important to recruit the best people possible for my team. The effort was sometimes significant, but after creating a great team, everything that followed was easier."

Foster Teamwork: "In collaborative projects that I worked on, such as going to Venus, teamwork is critical. Simple values such as meeting your commitments, showing up on time, saying what you are going to do, then doing what you said, are vital. Good leadership is properly valued. Good fellowship is undervalued. Creating an atmosphere of responsibility, respect, friendship, and a sense of common purpose were goals that I strived for. Humor also helped."

Strive for Excellence: "I worked hard, often seven days a week. I left the office when I got tired and not when the office hours had ended. I was on duty 24/7. I tried to the best of my ability to make everything—technology, business, and teamwork—as good as possible."

Steven D. Dorfman Biography

Steven D. Dorfman is the retired vice chairman of Hughes Electronics. During his time at Hughes, he served as CEO of Hughes Space and Communications Company, the world's leading builder of communication satellites and a provider of Space Systems for the NASA, NRO, navy, and air force; Hughes Communications, a leading owner and operator of communication satellites; and Hughes Telecommunications and Space, a unit responsible for the above businesses plus the international development of DirecTV.

While CEO of Hughes Communications, Dorfman was responsible for the development of the Galaxy System, the leading North American satellite service provider, subsequently merged with Intelsat; the JCSAT system for Japan, in partnership with Mitsui and Itochu; the initiation of the direct-to-home business at Hughes, which ultimately became DirecTV; and several other satellite businesses. Earlier in his career, Dorfman was responsible for space exploration at Hughes, including planetary exploration, weather and scientific satellites, and mapping of earth resources from space. He managed the Pioneer Venus program, which landed five probes on the surface of Venus.

After retiring from Hughes, Mr. Dorfman was the Hunsaker visiting professor at MIT, the chairman of ProtoStar Ltd., and a member of the President's Information Technology Advisory Committee.

Mr. Dorfman has served on the boards of Hughes, Raytheon, PanAmSat, American Mobile Satellite, Galaxy Latin America, JCSAT, DirecTV, Galaxy Institute, ProtoStar, and HRL Laboratories. He has been a trustee of the Boys and Girls Club and the Devereux Foundation. He is currently a member of the National Academy of Engineering (NAE), the Tennenbaum Capital Advisory Board, the Thoroughbred Owners of California, and the California Lutheran University School of Management Advisory Board and is a senior fellow of the California Council for Science and Technology. He has served on advisory committees for NASA, FCC, USIA, Department of Transportation, air force, USC School of Engineering, Hughes Network Systems, Boeing Satellite Systems, JPL, Ames Research Center, and the National Research Council.

Among Mr. Dorfman's awards are the Distinguished Public Service Award, NASA's highest award, for his work on Pioneer Venus; the Society of Satellite Professionals Hall of Fame; and Via Satellite's Satellite Executive of the Year for 1995. He has received an honorary doctor of science degree from Morgan State University.

Chapter 4

John Bardgette, Exxon-Former Executive, Former Senior Project Manager, 3 World Records

John Bardgette and his wife

Former Exxon Executive, Senior Project Manager, Civil Engineer, and Holder of Three World Records for Largest Oil Platforms Built

The Importance of Team Building on an International Basis

The pilot was skillfully maneuvering the sleek, shiny helicopter through a beautiful high-blue Pacific Ocean sky. The chopper slowly circled the massive offshore platform under which the peaceful Pacific waters rolled.

The chopper landed softly on the platform floor, and shortly afterwards, a door opened, and a tall, rugged Texan emerged. This imposing man strode confidently across the platform, absorbing his surroundings, which were a source of pride and joy. He was one of Exxon's elite. He was miles away from the safety and comfort of the corporate office towers. But Exxon relied on his courage, unlimited knowledge, and willingness to go into the trenches to protect its product worldwide. Its product is one of the world's most precious resources. It is a resource over which wars have been fought for decades. Poets and songwriters call it "black gold." We are talking oil!

Who is this elite oil guru? His name is John Bardgette. As Bardgette surveys his work and he walks along the huge platform, his pride increases in intensity. The size of the project was monumental, since the overall height of the platform "legs," or jackets as they are called, measure approximately one hundred yards tall or approximately the length of a football field. He felt this emotion because he had led and supervised the team at Exxon that allowed this project to become a major success. The Hondo platform on which he stood is one of the largest oil offshore platforms that has ever been constructed, and at the time construction was completed, it held a Guinness world record by doubling the previous water-depth record of a platform. Bardgette's mind flashes back to the enormity of this project, in regard to civil engineering, construction, resources required, innovation in technology, and tens of thousands of labor hours, which took years and a vast set of capital expenditures. From the beginning to the end of this monumental project, the risk for failure was high indeed for the oil giant Exxon.

In the pages that follow, you will learn about this man. We will examine the different influences that shaped this talented individual. We will discover his values. We will listen to his advice. We will hear testimonies about his skills and abilities from a variety of voices.

Success stories can be both entertaining and instructive. I think you will find the following story of John Bardgette to be unquestionably both.

Major Accomplishments at Exxon—Forty-Three-Year Career in Civil Engineering Hondo Project

John Bardgette is a man who thrived at Exxon as a senior project manager for over forty-three years, building three of the world's largest offshore drilling and production platforms. His tenacity and capacity for leading others are exemplary, and his accomplishments while at Exxon are the stuff of legend. As Bardgette surveyed his work and the work of countless other employees on this oil platform where he was standing, his mind flashed back to the origins of this work.

This tremendous project was called the Hondo Project by Exxon, which means "deep" in Spanish. Bardgette recalled that the Hondo Project started when the Bureau of Land Management opened up lease options for a 110 track of the Pacific Ocean to be developed for oil excavation and production. Exxon committed $218 million in 1968 to acquire the lease for forty-seven tracks in the Santa Barbara Channel. This parcel was the equivalent of 83,000 acres and combined the eighteen leases of Exxon with five Shell and Chevron leases. Exxon would be the operator of the entire operation.

John Bardgette continued to reflect on the beginning of the strategic plan of the Hondo Project as he stood and watched the tumultuous waves escalate underneath the oil platform. He recalled that Exxon selected two strategic operations to enable oil production from this site on the Pacific coast. The first strategic operation was to construct an onshore treating facility, and the second strategic operation would be to construct and "to utilize an offshore storage and treating vessel (OS&T) connected to a single anchor leg mooring (SALM), and 8,500 feet from the Hondo platform."[1] All of the oil wells would be directionally drilled.

Bardgette would also go on to remember the complex nature of this feat. "The Hondo platform set a water depth world record for a platform connected to the ocean floor (a fixed platform). It would be constructed and immersed in 850 feet of water, and at the time of installation, the deepest water depth for a fixed platform was 476 feet in the North Sea. When completed, the Honda platform with the drilling derrick would measure 1,143 feet from the ocean floor to the top of the drilling derrick. This was nearly as tall as the Empire State Building (1,454 feet) and taller than San Francisco's Trans America Tower (850 feet)."[2] Also, the enormity of this project could be emphasized by the former record of ocean floor fixed platforms as being close to half the depth, as 476 feet in the North Sea compared to the projection of the Hondo Project as being

---

[1] John Bardgette autobiography, chapter 20, page 1.
[2] John Bardgette autobiography, chapter 20, page 1.

850 feet in oceanic depth. The success of the completion of this project with tremendous risk was a great triumph for Exxon, John Bardgette, and their employees. As Bardgette recollects, he is very proud of the world-breaking record of the platform depth to the ocean floor and completion of the project with high safety standards, with no serious injuries to the employees or contractors. They were also successful in coming in close to their original budget of $80 million, which today, based on inflation, would be a number that would have exceeded $1 billion.

Before the construction started, Bardgette became the project manager of the Hondo Project, and he and his staff projected a budget of $80 million, and that budget was approved. However, he is most proud of the tremendous effort of his team and the countless individuals who contributed to this project. Bardgette goes on to briefly explain the formation of the Hondo Platform, and editorial content will also be used from a videotape entitled *Beyond the Shores—Hondo*.

The Hondo platform project was largely based on five stages:

- the engineering, research, and design of the structure
- the fabrication of the jacket, which required over 12,000 tons of steel
- the assembly and construction of the structure
- the final installation of the structure in the Pacific Ocean in 850 feet of ocean depth
- the drilling of twenty-eight wells from the Hondo platform that set a world record for a petroleum drilling and production platform

Hondo—Engineering, Construction, and Installation of the Project Hondo Engineering and Design

John Bardgette first met with Arthur Lee Guy, the chief design engineer in charge of platform design at the Humble Oil Company, to gain insight about the feasibility of this project and the constraints of delivering the structure to its final destination. This delivery of the Hondo platform was a big factor since, due to the overall dimensions, certain ocean and port conditions would prohibit the transport of this huge structure. Thus the two men quickly "concluded that the jacket would be too wide to pass through the Panama Canal locks, and that towing this large jacket around the tip of South America would be too hazardous. This led to a jacket design with two segments, and the segments would be connected at the site, using large flanges. John Bardgette proposed that hydro-flanges and stabbing cones be used, which would be more efficient and would provide a more accurate alignment while joining the two segments at sea."[3] The two segments were designed with four legs that would be towed individually. The two segments were joined while floating in the Santa Barbara Channel in a horizontal position, and then towed to the planned location and upended by controlled flooding in the legs. This process would eliminate any transportation constraints.

"The structure of the Hondo platform was designed and engineered with eight legs, which were 54 inches in diameter and 850 feet tall. These legs would be interconnected with bracings and twelve skirt pile sleeves, which are 63 inches in diameter. Once the platform substructure was in place in the ocean, twenty steel piles were driven with depths ranging from 250 to 375 feet deep into the ocean floor. These pilings would serve to secure the platform in place."[4] "The earthquake criteria controlled the structural design of most of the jackets and joints. However, with one of Bardgette's patented designs, this was made more structurally sound by what he called a "jacket crown connector" that had also been used on one of Exxon's Gulf of Mexico platforms."[5]

Above the ocean surface, the deck units were installed on top of the legs, and a drilling derrick was set on top of the deck. This extended the overall height to be 1,143 feet above the ocean floor and 293 feet above the water line. From the new platform, Exxon would drill twenty-eight wells. The wells would be drilled to an average measured depth of 11,000 feet and directionally drilled extending out to be as far as 8,000 feet from under the platform. The technology of developing, designing, and building the world's tallest offshore oil platform was monumental both in concept and scope. To meet these challenges, Exxon engineers, scientists, platform experts, and over forty consultants designed a production platform using

---

[3] John Bardgette autobiography, chapter 20.
[4] *Beyond the Shores—Hondo* videotape.
[5] John Bardgette autobiography, chapter 20.

the most advanced technology. John Bardgette was the project manager of Hondo.

Hondo Construction on Land

Bardgette and his team would set the following directives for this project. The platform deck sections and pilings were constructed and fabricated in Morgan City, Louisiana, by Exxon's primary contracting company for the project, J Ray McDermott Construction Company. Kaiser Steel Corporation assembled the jackets for the project in Oakland, California. Tubular subassemblies were fabricated in Napa and Fontana, California. Kaiser Steel Mill was largely responsible for manufacturing over 12,000 tons of steel for the jacket alone. The steel plates were then delivered to their plants in Napa and Fontana for fabrication, where they were rolled into tubular sections. The jacket was then assembled at Kaiser's Oakland yard on the San Francisco Bay, which was one of the few locations with water frontage on the West Coast that would be large enough for the fabrication of such a monumental project. The leg assembly would be constructed just above the ground in a horizontal manner and then upon completion be hoisted up by gigantic cranes. These frames or legs were approximately 215 to 365 feet long and were 54 inches in diameter. Once all eight legs were hoisted up, they would then be connected by steel pipe, X-joint bracing. "A unique element was the ball-type joint for intersecting pipe of X jacket framing members, where two pipes appeared to pass through each other,"[6] further providing extra stability and reinforcement. This new design would also be patented by Exxon.

Hondo—Transport and Installation Phase at Sea

Once the construction land phase was complete, Bardgette and his Exxon team would implement the oceanic transportation phase. The first and lower section of the jacket, weighing 7,000 tons, would be carefully loaded onto a barge, *Oceanic 93*, using a hydraulic jacking system, which took

---

[6] John Bardgette autobiography, chapter 20.

approximately twenty-four hours. After the loading was complete, 175 steel pipe braces were welded to the jacket and the barge deck to secure it for the tow. The load out of the lower jacket was completed on May 21, 1976, one year after the start of the construction.

The voyage of each jacket section through the Pacific Ocean would be potentially perilous were it not for the two oceangoing tugs and six harbor tugs that were used from Kaiser dock to the Golden Gate Bridge. From there, the two oceangoing tugs towed the launch barge to Santa Barbara Channel. The jacket, laying on its side as it was being towed, would measure 192 feet tall above the water surface after it was installed. The route would originate in Oakland, passing under the Oakland Bay Bridge, with a clearance of twenty-eight feet, as well as passing under the San Francisco Golden Gate Bridge with a clearance of forty feet. The voyage of the lower jacket would end at the Santa Barbara Channel in California and be launched from the barge into the ocean. The lower jacket would be tied to another derrick barge, named derrick barge 12, and would be held at that location until the upper jacket arrived. The derrick barge *Oceanic 93* would make its way back to the original site and return to pick up the upper jacket, which was still waiting at the Oakland yard. As the upper jacket traveled through the waters toward the lower jacket, it would soon make its destination, which was approximately ten feet from the lower jacket. It would also be secured by another barge. The next monumental task would be to join the upper jacket to the lower jacket; both were on top of the water waiting to be mounted. The jackets were pulled together by a winch, the stabbing cones were fully engaged, the hydro-flanges were aligned, and an underwater remote vehicle confirmed that the underwater flanges were also properly engaged and aligned. This was all done under the perilous condition of the rough sea conditions. After the hydro-flanges were in the proper place, the rubber gaskets were compressed, making the chamber watertight.

The caps on the access tubes were removed, and the water that had been trapped inside was then blown out. As the eight chambers became dry, individual McDermott welders were then lowered into the chambers. The distance for the welders to be lowered into the chambers measured 110 feet below the ocean surface. The welding of the chambers was dangerous but successful, and the two jacket structures, both the upper and the lower jackets, were joined.

The next operation involved towing the entire structure to another location approximately thirty miles away toward Santa Barbara. Upon the arrival of the structure to its destination, the sleeves of the jackets were flooded, which would naturally submerge the lower portion of the jacket. These were flooded until the structure would be upright in a vertical position, and finally underwater cameras were used to confirm that the jacket was correctly positioned to meet the slope of the ocean floor.

Next, the caps, or the tops of the four jacket legs, were cut off, and the pilings would soon be driven from the top of the jacket legs, through the legs, and into the Santa Barbara Channel floor. The piles were driven by a large steam-driven hammer, which at the time was the largest steam hammer manufactured in the United States. The piles were fabricated in Morgan City, Louisiana, and were towed through the Panama Canal to Port Hueneme, a 5,000-mile distance. Eight piles were driven in each of the eight jacket legs and were drilled into the ocean with a penetration of 375 feet and a diameter per pile of 48 inches. Twelve additional piles measuring 54 inches were driven through the skirt pile sleeves to an oceanic depth of 250 feet. Thus a total of twenty piles were driven into the ocean floor, and twenty-eight additional conductor pipes measuring 20 inches in diameter were driven to a penetration of 200 feet for oil excavation purposes.

For the completion of this Hondo Project, deck units would be partially fabricated at the McDermott fabrication yard in New Orleans and transported through the Panama Canal. The enormous size of the decks limited the completion of the decks, and the fabrication was completed in Port Hueneme. They were then towed to the platform installation site and installed along with the drilling rig, the emergency flare boom, cranes, and the quarters building.

John Bardgette once again reflects on the enormity of this project as he stands on the completed platform and marvels at the success of all of the completed phases. He continues to have tremendous pride in his team at Exxon and the world records that this platform achieved. These achievements were all accomplished within the time frame and the budget that he and his Exxon team calculated in their original business model for Hondo.

A Village of Knowledge

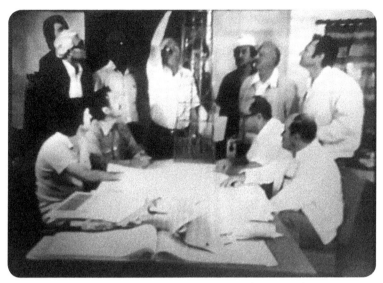

John Bardgette and his Exxon team at work on Hondo Project

John Bardgette at work on Hondo Project

Hondo construction site—Oakland

Hondo platform towed in Pacific Ocean

Japan—Iwaki Project—Exxon

As John Bardgette continues to reflect on the collection of his peak career moments as an executive at Exxon, he fondly recalls the highly important Iwaki Project in Japan. Another world-record-breaking project that Bardgette oversaw at Exxon as project manager was the Iwaki platform, which was located 140 miles north of Tokyo. This oil platform, which was located twenty-five miles offshore in the Pacific Ocean, set a world record by being installed in one of the most seismically active regions in the world, prone to earthquakes. This project was another highly complex one, which Bardgette would find to be tremendously challenging and rewarding. As Exxon continued to depend on the tremendous leadership capabilities of John Bardgette as a project manager, they put him in charge of more complex projects, which was the nature of this Iwaki platform in Japan.

As John Bardgette stated, "I didn't know it at the time, but by the time my job was complete, I thought of this as being my best project in my career at Exxon."[7] The Iwaki Project was such a challenging one due to the very nature of the location in conjunction with the seismic center, and the oil platform would need to be engineered to withstand an earthquake with a magnitude of 8.2. This tolerance for a high earthquake could also be seen in the nearby "Fukushima Daiichi Nuclear power plant. Tohoku Electric Power Company owned this plant, and a conventional coal-fired electric power plant almost directly onshore from the Iwaki platform. Tohoku Electric Power Company, or Toden as it is commonly called in Japan, converted one of their turbines to operate on natural gas that Esso provided from the Iwaki platform. The Iwaki Project consisted of a platform, an onshore natural gas processing plant, a pipeline from the platform to the gas processing plant, a special earthquake resistant drilling derrick, a heliport, and a dock modified to accommodate oil industry requirements. Unlike the United States, Japan was nearly devoid of infrastructure to meet oil industry needs."[8]

On August 7, 1981, John Bardgette and his wife, Jean, arrived at the Tokyo Airport to start in his role with this very important civil engineering

---

[7] John Bardgette autobiography, chapter 25.
[8] John Bardgette autobiography, chapter 25.

project. John Bardgette would soon meet with his boss, Leon Smith, general manager of Esso Production Japan (EJP), to officially begin his assignment as the project division manager for the Iwaki Project of Japan. Bardgette was introduced to "Ouchi-san, the Vice-President, and Senior Officer of EPJ, Yasuyuki Maki (Maki-san), advisor from Teikatu Oil Company/Offshore Iwaki Production, TOC/OIP, and all of the staff that had already arrived. Later Leon introduced him to Dale Owens, President of Esso Sekiyu. Maki-san became his travelling companion to all of the platform fabrication sites, and his best Japanese friend."[9] Esso Production Japan was a subsidiary of Esso Sekiyu.

John Bardgette soon toured the fabrication yard, where the platform jackets were being manufactured at the Hyundai Ulsan yard, and he quickly perceived that the jackets would not be completed within the necessary time frame of construction. He also believed that Esso did not have the adequate staffing for the project, and he believed that Esso should carry some of the blame in this slow pace of fabrication. At that time, there was only one engineer responsible for Hyundai's work. Bardgette knew that he and the EPJ team must move swiftly to divert catastrophic time constraints, and therefore, soon there would be a letter of cancellation for the contract sent to Chung Ju-yung, chairman of Hyundai. However, before the letter of cancellation was sent out, John Bardgette and his team wanted to confirm that Nippon Steel Corporation (NSC) would accept a contract based on their original bid for the construction of the Iwaki jacket. Nippon Steel agreed to their original bid but only after they were assured that Hyundai Heavy Industries (HHI) would not hold a grudge against Nippon Steel. This was based on the fact that Hyundai Heavy Industries was an important customer, and they did not want to jeopardize losing HHI's steel plates business. After this assurance was given, Nippon Steel would agree to construct the Iwaki jacket. A series of negotiations were worked out for this cancelled contract, and the fabricator Hyundai would accept another contract for a land phase fabrication of the platform components. This arrangement was acceptable to all parties, and this agreement was signed by all parties. After this agreement was settled, time continued to be a

---

[9] John Bardgette autobiography, chapter 25.

tremendous constraint, and therefore, upon revision of the contracts, the necessary staff had to be reorganized and filled.

The contract for the jacket fabrication was awarded to Nippon Steel Corporation (NSC) in November 1981, and the fabrication of the conductor pipes was awarded to Hyundai Heavy Industries (HHI) in 1982. Other subcontractors included NKK, which was contracted to construct the deck modules and the quarters building. MHI, MES, and IHI were also involved in subcontract work on the Iwaki Project.

John Bardgette reflected upon the enormity and complexity in using so many contractors and subcontractors. He believed that the Japanese government had used its influence to expand the scope of the work to multiple Japanese companies, further benefiting them with these contracts. Under normal circumstances, such as the Hondo Project, there would typically be two principal contractors. In the case of the Hondo Project, the principal contracts were contracted to McDermott and Kaiser Steel. McDermott had only one fabrication site and no subcontractors, and Kaiser Steel had three separate fabrication sites and only one assembly site. In the Iwaki Project, there were over twenty construction sites that required inspection work. John Bardgette explained that the construction sites spanned over a distance of a thousand miles, which included all of the four principal Japanese islands. In order to provide quality assurance on this massive project, the quality assurance, quality control (QA/QC), and inspection contract was awarded to Victoria Welding Supervision Company Ltd. (AWS), an Australian company for the inspection services at the construction and fabrication sites. This contract would serve to streamline the confirmation of quality testing over a broad geographical area in Japan to one company and give John Bardgette better capability of managing this complex project.

Originally when John Bardgette arrived in Tokyo, his staff was limited to one construction engineer and a secretary, Setsuko Soda San, who he would later adopt as his Japanese daughter. Soon after Bardgette's arrival to Japan, he increased his staff until it was the appropriate size to build and manage the Iwaki Project. The staff largely consisted of Esso/Exxon employees 60–70 percent, and the balance of those hired was outside of the company. On each of the hired employees, John Bardgette would review their resumes before they were hired.

The following engineers would be tremendously important to the success of this Iwaki Project. Bill Brill was assigned as the construction manager, and Rick Wood was assigned as the engineering manager. Both were long-term Exxon/Esso employees. Richard Burke was hired as the quality control manager. By the end of the year, twenty-four engineers, technicians, and secretaries had arrived from an international pool of talent from such geographical areas as Australia, Canada, the UK, Colombia, and the United States.

Meetings would be held once a month, and John Bardgette would meet with their three partner companies, Offshore Iwaki Petroleum Company (OIP), General Sekiyu Refining Company, and Tonnen Oil Marketing Company. Due to the Japanese language and communication between the executives during the meetings, there were multiple translators to ensure that the correct information was being transferred to the parties involved.

John Bardgette would make repeated visits to the construction yards that were fabricating the platform components. His visits to the onshore gas processing facility sites would be less frequent. As the project manager of the Iwaki Project, he would find these visits to be invaluable for firsthand knowledge of progress and enable him to pass on his engineering expertise to those young engineers who were relatively new to this level and complexity of construction.

To put the differences between the Hondo Project off of the coast of California and the Iwaki Project off of the coast of Japan in perspective, one could first analyze the size of the jackets for each project. The jackets for the Hondo Project weighed 12,000 tons, and the jackets for the Iwaki Project would weigh 15,000 tons.

As John Bardgette described in his autobiography, "both Kaiser's Oakland yard and NSC's Wakamatsu yard required significant preparation before assembly could start. Both built pile supported skidways topped with Teflon. NSC did require a lot of assistance from EPJ. Yard preparation work took several weeks. While this was in progress Kaiser completed some shop drawings and started fabrication of components at two of their other facilities, and NSC did likewise at three of their subcontractors. After the skidways were completed, assembly of the components started, using conventional methods. The jacket sections were built lying horizontal, or parallel to and above the ground. There was one exception to conventional procedures used on a smaller jacket; this change was pioneered on Hondo jacket. The interior jacket sections were rolled up and secured with guy lines above the skidways on sand-jacks. The Iwaki jacket bents were fabricated in two sections for roll-ups and welded together after they were vertical, and secured with guy cables. The first roll up was on June 15, 1982, and work proceeded smoothly, with the last roll-up October 28, 1982. NSC was efficient in maintaining their schedule for the 18-month fabrication schedule. NSC's yard manager, Ebina San, was very good at scheduling all of the off-site fabrication to arrive at Wakamatsu as needed."[10] During the entire jacket construction, the project stayed remarkably close to the planned schedule.

Through the manufacturing process, John Bardgette would discover that there were certain issues regarding the engineering quality control of two main parts, which were dimensional controls and protective coatings of the jackets. Most of the contractor's past expertise had been based on shipbuilding. In shipbuilding, much thinner pieces of steel were welded together compared to the thicker welding plates that were required for the jackets installed on the Iwaki platform. These contractors also lacked the knowledge of the welding plate's shrinkage and the possible corrosion of the traps, where corrosive water could stand from the oceanic waters. John Bardgette fully believed "that construction of all topsides components, module support frame, production modules, drilling modules, and minor components, would have proceeded with less problems if Exxon had furnished completely designed facilities, and if EPJ had provided, in the contracts, that all required welding procedures be essentially complete before any fabrication started."[11] He would continue to explain that the fabrication managers they worked with were average as compared to those who worked in the United States companies, and he attributed that to the Japanese work culture and the absences of unions in Japan.

---

[10] John Bardgette autobiography, chapter 25.

[11] John Bardgette autobiography, chapter 25.

Completed Jackets Loaded onto Barges to Travel to the Iwaki Oceanic Project Site

Upon completion of the jackets, the jackets were loaded on the Heerema's 109 launch barge and towed approximately a thousand miles by two tugboats to the launch site. The arrival date of the jackets was May 6, 1983, which was six days later. Heerema's derrick barge *Thor* was ready for its arrival of the jackets. With tremendous rotating capacity of 1,600 tons and a fixed over-the-stern capacity of two thousand, the *Thor* was fully capable to take the load from Heerema 109. However, due to bad weather conditions, Heerema had to wait for three days to ballast the launch barge.

John Bardgette described the beautiful scene on the day of the launch: "I was standing on the deck of the Thor on that morning and I had a beautiful view of the base of the jacket as it was launched with the sun rising behind it, about 4:00AM on March 10. The jacket, setting on the ocean floor, was about two-feet higher than planned, and a few inches out of level. This was within acceptable limits. Later when the platform installation was essentially complete, the boat landing had to be lowered."[12]

The Completion of the Iwaki Project

The completion of the Iwaki Project had many hurdles and obstacles to overcome, but the timeline and budget for completion went largely according to scheduling and budgeting requirements. The following events occurred to complete the Iwaki Project. This same series of events is required for all offshore projects:

- Piles were driven using Menck single-acting steam hammers.
- Skirt piles were driven with a Menck hydraulic underwater hammer.
- The pile-to-jacket connections were made.
- A twenty-foot column of grout was pumped in the bottom of the pile-shirt sleeve annulus and allowed to set.
- The conductor pipe was driven.

---

[12] John Bardgette autobiography, chapter 25.

- The field connections of the production facilities were started.
- Welding and painting work was completed.
- NKK completed the process facility work and also the drilling rig installation work.
- A pilot hole was drilled from shore.
- The 4,000-foot section of pipe was attached to the drill pipe.
- The pipe was successfully pulled through the borehole.
- The lay barge had laid pipe at the platform and pulled it up through the j-tube with a winch.
- The end of the pipe protruding from the borehole was raised above the water surface.
- The pipe was welded to the pipeline from the platform.
- The pipe was then laid back on the ocean floor in a gentle curve.
- A plow was then used to bury the pipeline.
- Finally the pipeline was pigged and tested. All pipeline work was completed in November 1983.
- The drilling staff had started assembling the drilling rig.
- The drilling modules were completed by July, and the skid base was completed by August, and this work was completed in January 1984.
- The first well was spudded before the end of the month.

Values and Principles of Leadership by John Bardgette

1. One cannot overemphasize the importance of building teams to provide success in the work environment.
2. Empower your employees and give them the support they need to fulfill successfully their personal and organizational goals. Take time to encourage them and treat them with the utmost respect.
3. Throughout life, both on a professional and a personal basis, integrity, honesty, and high ethical standards should govern your behavior.
4. Understanding your end goal as a manager is critical, and understanding the business strategy for accomplishing this end goal is of inestimable value.

5. Always maintain flexibility by having a willingness to adapt policy and strategy as new information becomes available.

John Bardgette's Comments On World Records Set During His Exxon Career

1. Humble Oil's (Exxon's) Gulf of Mexico West Delta 73A platform in 180 feet of water, exceeding the existing record of a fixed platform in 146 feet in the North Sea.
2. Exxon's Santa Barbara Channel Hondo platform in 850 feet of water, exceeding the existing record of a fixed platform in 475 feet in the North Sea. Welders working in a dry chamber 110 feet below the surface of the water probably set a world record.
3. Exxon's Santa Barbara Channel **single anchor leg mooring** (SALM) set four world records. It was in 490 feet of water. I don't have the water depth of existing SALMs but know that they were much less, about 100 feet to 250 feet. It was the first SALM installed in US waters. Its electrical power swivel was the largest slip ring ever built and the only one designed for high amperage and high voltage. The connections of the three pipelines from the Hondo platform to the base of the SALM was done by divers working from a hyperbaric chamber in the deepest water and for the longest period of time by commercial divers. Only the navy's divers had worked in deeper water, and only for short periods of time.
4. Esso Japan's Iwaki platform was installed in the most seismically active area that any platform had been installed in. I believe that this record still stands.
5. Exxon's **Santa Ynez Unit** (SYU) Project had two huge platforms, Harmony and Heritage. Harmony's jacket weighted 44,100 tons, and Heritage's jacket weighted 35,500 tons. Each of these were transported across the Pacific Ocean to Santa Barbara Channel, a distance of about 6,900 nautical miles, on *Heerema*'s new launch barge *H-853*. To the best of my knowledge, this was the longest tow of any platform jacket and in harsh weather conditions. I believe this set a world record.

To put this in perspective, *Heerema*'s *H-853* was capable of carrying a load of 60,000 tons, large enough to carry the USA's carrier *Nimitz*.

Exxon Record

Exxon's SYU Project Harmony platform in 12,000 feet of water exceeded their Gulf of Mexico tower in one thousand feet of water. This platform would have set a world record had it not been delayed several times for labor unrest at Hyundai's fabrication yard, a permitting problem with Santa Barbara County, and Exxon's temporary cash flow concern. Due to these delays, Shell's Cognac platform was installed in 13,000 feet of water in the Gulf of Mexico about two months before Exxon's Harmony platform.

Accolades for John Bardgette

The following section presents a sample of the many accolades and tributes that are found in chapter 28 of John Bardgette's autobiography. These comments provide illumination that is helpful in seeing the extraordinary, admirable qualities of this remarkable man. Here are grateful attitudes and high opinions communicated to Bardgette at the time of his retirement and afterwards. They span the time frame from 1998 to 2014. What better empirical evidence of the talents, knowledge, and abilities of John Bardgette than the words of those men and women closely associated with him who had the opportunity to observe his behavior in a variety of circumstances.

M.O. "Pat" Pattison wrote: "As you reach the time of retirement, I want to extend my congratulations for a long, loyal, and rewarding career. Very few people have, or have had the opportunity to do what you have done.

"To be able to say, 'I have done what has never before been done,' does not happen to many. When I think of the 'Hondo' platform I am reminded and amazed by your experiences with 'Annie' on the derrick barge, and why she should not spend the night on board with a couple hundred men."

(Pat was one of two of the best bosses that I had. He was my boss twice—once when he was division civil engineer in the Eastern Division, and when he was division civil engineer in the Western Division. —John Bardgette)

Bob Haring wrote: "Congratulations on a memorable career which has touched so many in the civil/construction side of Exxon's business. You can truly say you have 'seen it all.'

"Not only have your protégés gone on to bigger and better things, but you have helped keep us research types straight on what is really important in the field. We will always be grateful for the strong support you provide for the introduction of 'science' (in the form of pile-driving instrumentation) into offshore construction, and for your support of our foundation support in general."

Scott Preston wrote: "The contributions you made to Exxon over the past 43 years are small in comparison to the contributions you've made to the men and women who worked with you. You challenged us; treated us fairly yet firmly; and respected our opinions. Having left Exxon near the end of the Iwaki project, I took with me many of your values and ideas, which have benefited me in my career with BP Exploration. I consider it my privilege to have worked for you and a greater honor to call you my friend."

Cindy Hewitt wrote: "Too often we don't verbalize our feelings about the people in our lives. This occasion has caused me to reflect on my association with you, John, and I wanted to take a few minutes to make sure you knew how much I appreciated everything you have done for me. It is truly rare to find a supervisor who inspires you to reach the highest level of performance possible. You were always demanding, but you never expected more from us than you were committing yourself. You encouraged me, consoled me, prodded me, and appreciated me. Although I wasn't officially in the SYU *(Santa Ynez Unit)* group, you included me in your planning and goals, and took the time to keep me informed of the project's successes and roadblocks.

"Working with you was a joy—you would give me an objective, and allow me to find a way to accomplish it, providing whatever support or guidance I needed. Best of all, you had confidence in my ability to contribute to the project, and you made me feel like part of the family.

"I always admired your energy, results-orientation, and tremendous tenacity. No matter what obstacles stood in your way, you persisted until you found a way to overcome them. I hope I have developed a fraction of the flexibility and dedication that you have displayed through your career at Exxon.

"Beyond our work relationship, I have always felt a special closeness to you. You showed a great interest in me as a person, as well as an employee. In many ways, I felt closer to you than I did to my own father. Please accept my best wishes to you and Jean for a happy and healthy retirement. Take care of each other."

Brian Grundmeier wrote: "Unforgettable! Inspiring! Suspenseful! Challenging! These are the words that will always come to my mind when reflecting on the work I've shared with you these past 5 years on the SYU project. During this time you've made quite an impression on me and taught some important lessons that will last my entire career.

"I'll also remember with admiration and respect: your ability to inspire the best work in people and instill pride in the work being done; your patience during technical presentations followed by probing questions and shrewd insight; your sense of history, and interest in and application for major feats accomplished by our civil engineering profession; and your willingness to teach young engineers important lessons from your experiences.

"(I've also noted your ability to strike fear (terror?) in the hearts of engineers from time to time! And your feats of world travel without any apparent jet lag are legendary.)

"I have truly enjoyed working under you and will always have good memories of these past 5 years together on the SYU project. Thanks a million."

Bill Brill wrote: "… let me take chance to THANK YOU for all the time and love you devoted to me during the 80's. I use many of the things you taught me every day. We really had our moments in a few meetings."

Virginia Gean, MBA, CMA

(I believe that Bill is reflecting on a meeting we had the day he got back from a vacation trip a few days late. I had out inquires to locate him. I was truly concerned that something could have happened to him. But he thought that I was unhappy with him. From his comment above, he must have later realized that I was really concerned about him. —John Bardgette)

Dick Raines wrote: "Thanks for the opportunity to work on some very interesting projects. One thing I'll remember is that you always gave me the opportunity to voice my opinion—even when you knew what I was going to say."

Walt Gray wrote: "Exxon, Western Division, has had a special image to us because of your presence and leadership. It was always obvious to us that you were setting a tone of fairness and open-mindedness while being firm on Exxon's needs and desires.

"You provided opportunities for the smaller companies to prove that we could make a contribution to Exxon's needs that resulted in good values to you. And this was consistently within an environment that was friendly and constructive, it has been a special privilege to work with you and the SYU organization."

(Walt was the owner of two companies, Gray Management & Engineering and Driverless Systems. We became close friends. —John Bardgette)

Cliff Barnett wrote: "John, my association with you over many years is very special to me. It has brought about a deep appreciation and admiration of you professionally and a proud, enjoyable feeling of friendship personally."

(Cliff was the senior partner of Barnett & Cesarean. —John Bardgette)

Lane Phillips wrote: "You have had what I know was an interesting and challenging career in the offshore industry, not just watching, but significantly participating in the growth from those early days out of Grand Isle to large, deep water mega projects like SYU. I consider it very fortunate to have participated in both your Iwaki and SYU projects, and I am grateful for those opportunities."

(Lane was an independent consultant. —John Bardgette)

Excerpt from James Theisen's October 26, 1998 letter: "I trust you are doing well and think of you often—the best 'boss' I ever had (I am sure I never told you enough how much I appreciated the way you worked with your associates and the opportunities for pay advancements you supported me with)."

Excerpt from Harry Longwell's, May 22, 2007, letter: "John, I've always held you in high regards for your integrity, attention to detail, and being one heck of a platform designer and constructor. You have made many contributions in your field to the company over your long, successful career and have provided the foundation that has allowed the company to be at the forefront of industry in offshore technology and exploration. I have told you this before, but I just wanted to say it again less either of us has forgotten it."

(Harry was one of two best bosses I had. He was my boss two times, when he was the offshore district engineer in the Eastern Division, and when he was Western Division manager when I was project manager of the Hondo Project. He was senior vice president, next to the CEO/chairman when he retired. —John Bardgette)

(During a conversation with Ron Fry, shortly after he was appointed project manager of the Syncrude Project in Canada, in June 2009, he told me that he was modeling his project management on my management style on the Iwaki and SYU projects. —John Bardgette)

Quotes from several e-mails from Ron Fry: "As far as 1984, you got me assigned to the Drilling Team after we finished the offshore installation, working as a subsurface engineer—I was always thankful for that experience—it certainly opened my eyes to the (very different) world of Drilling. A big help as my career progressed. The conductor pipes went in offshore like butter—no issues whatsoever—it was a very wise move to have the rig do this, a good lesson learned."

Excerpts from Ron Fry's 2012–2014 e-mails: "I must admit it was quite overwhelming to be working for the great Mr. John Bardgette, but as I would come to learn, you really did take care of your entire Team in Tokyo, in a very personal, kind and caring way."

"One of the many things I learned from you as a mentor, and one that I always followed in my career as well—people are our most important asset (and take care of everyone!)."

"On the project side, believe it was the normal contract closeout activities, plus what sticks out for me were the individual project final reports that you had each of your teams write—Topsides, Jacket, Pipeline, Onshore, Offshore, etc. I still have the complete set of those very professional blue binders in my attic in Houston—one of the few things I kept after retirement. They were especially well done, best I had ever seen at the time (and not topped in my career)."

"John Nowadly was in town this week, and Yarami *(Pena)* and I *(Ron Fry)* had dinner with him. Was very enjoyable, reliving the days in Ulsan, and basking in what we were able to accomplish with HHI. We really did have a good team! I still stay in touch with J.D. Kim of HHI (he was a young engineer on SYU, and is now a Sr. VP), and he says when he looks back, SYU was really a great learning experience for HHI, and he gives Exxon a lot of credit for helping to turn HHI into the world's best fabricator. John *(Nowadly)* and Yarami *(Pena)* recalled the late VRA *(Voluntary Restraint Agreement)* on the Topsides, and their trip to Seoul, and then the later briefing with John Bardgette, who pounded the table and called it a 'nit'! Not sure if you remember the meeting, but John and Yarami clearly got your message! And of course all three of us thanked John Bardgette for what he helped us accomplish in our careers."

"Thanks for sharing your background, I feel very honored. And it seems to me that some of those hardships may have helped develop you into the kind, caring, and very considerate man I met on Iwaki. At first, I must admit it was quite overwhelming to be working for the great Mr. John Bardgette, but as I would come to learn, you really did take care of your entire Team in Tokyo, in a very personal, kind and caring way. And it was genuine, from the heart. Just one of the many things I learned from you as a mentor, and one that I always followed in my career as well—people are our most important asset (and take care of everyone!)."

John Nowadly's e-mail states: "Best of luck on the autobiography. When I was there, *(Ulsan, Korea)* I knew the SYU Korea team was outstanding in technical, professional, interpersonal, and so many other attributes, but it wasn't until years later with exposure to many more projects, teams, and individuals that I came to realize how truly outstanding and unique our team was. Consistent with that, I have come to appreciate much more what an outstanding effort it was on the part of you and the rest of EUSA leadership to assemble, assimilate, and support such a team. Thanks again for that great opportunity and memory."

John Hofferber's e-mail states: "Exxon has been treating me well. A few years ago, they opened the door for a few folks on the Technical ladder to enter the Executive Ranks. So I am currently holding the most senior technical position in the Company in construction of major capital projects (it's no wonder, given the roots I have under the Goleta Gang over 33 years ago)." *(The Goleta Gang was the Hondo Project staff.)*

John Plugge's e-mail states: "I just competed year 32 with EM and have been in my current role a little over 3 years. EMDC is extremely active with over 30 projects in execution and EMWI capex *(capital expenditure)* for the last two years approx. $17b. Oh what you used to be able to build for a few hundred million dollars. On SYU, I was fortunate to work on several pieces of the project missing out pipeline. Stated with 4 years in Korea which you may recall then went to build the 2 living quarters at Laport Contractors in Channelview Texas. I went from there to build the topsides at Gulf Marine in Aransas Pass and followed offshore for hookup and Flores plant thru startup. This was the first of several large projects I have enjoyed and I earned a lot about the project business on SYU."

E-mail from Joe Liles, SYU project manager: "John I have always have had the utmost respect for you and your management skills."

(Joe was general manager of the SYU Project. —John Bardgette)

Excerpt from a conversation with Robin Robinson in July 1984, shortly before Bardgette departed Japan for the SYU Project: "At the end of my meeting with Robin he told me that I was the smartest man that he had ever had the pleasure of supervising. I smiled and thanked him for his kind words." —John Bardgette

(Robin was the general manager of the Iwaki Project, my boss. —John Bardgette)

Excerpts from Carl Bender's July 7, 1987 letter: "This letter is to request your assistance in reestablishing a reference list of Production Department technical experts. Let me explain what we mean by 'expert.' We feel that there are at least two kinds of experts. One, which we might call first echelon experts, are those individuals who possess an exceptionally high level of expertise, and in all probability are recognized both inside and outside the Company for their expertise. For example, you yourself are one such expert in the Civil/Construction area in the opinion of our subcommittee. We probably have only a few first echelon experts in the Production Department and in some areas of technology, may have none at all."

Excerpt from Bob Rugeley's August 18, 1987 letter: "Having been associated with you has been real honor for me. I have the utmost respect for your professional capabilities and express my thanks for your past help, advice and wise counsel. In my opinion, your knowledge and capabilities in construction is unsurpassed in Exxon."

(Bob was Eastern Division civil engineering for a short time. —John Bardgette)

Excerpt from a conversation with A.L. Guy in September 2005 following Hurricane Katrina, one of the strongest hurricanes to strike Louisiana and the many platforms in the Gulf of Mexico: "A.L. called to tell me that none of Exxon's platforms had sustained any major damage, only walkways below the decks." —John Bardgette

(He was complimenting both of us; he had been in charge of designing them, and I had been in charge of building them. This hurricane destroyed or severely damaged thirty platforms, including destroying one of Shell Oil Company's platforms. I had always thought that Shell was Exxon's main competitor for quality of offshore platforms. —John Bardgette)

It is clear that respect, gratitude, and profound admiration are threaded throughout all the testimonies above. All these voices seem to be saying collectively that John Bardgette as a leader was tough with ideas but tender with people.

Chapter 5

Craig Zobelein, Hughes- Former Aerospace Engineer and 7 Other Careers

Craig Zobelein

Hughes Aerospace Electrical Engineer and Seven Other Inspiring Occupations

Live Life with Passion!

Find Your Treasure within and Develop the Talents That Will Bring You Satisfaction

To be in the same room with Craig Zobelein, one immediately recognizes that he is a true force of nature, a whirlwind, with a combination of energy, enthusiasm, humor, and passion. As he gave a lecture to one of my classes, much to my amazement, he had the students in the palm of his hand. As he showed off his dancing skills by circling in pirouettes, the class was laughing and could feel his enthusiasm for life. Zobelein's personality was infectious, and he brought tremendous energy to the room. He was a true entertainer and having a ball telling stories about his life.

The story of his life is an amazing one. He described his childhood. He said that he had a breakthrough idea when he, at the tender age of ten years old, realized that he did not want his life to be saddled with debt. Zobelein understood in his youth that life should be lived to the fullest and that he would want to do exactly what he wanted to do in his professional career, and do it with single-minded passion. It is very rare to hear of a child having that much foresight, but Zobelein lives his life to the fullest and has been able to go wherever his dreams and passions take him. Largely due to the result of managing risk, this philosophy enabled Zobelein to choose careers that would inspire and excite him. He explained his financial strategy: "I knew at a very early age that I wanted to retire at age forty-five and have all of my debt paid off, which would include my home mortgage, my automobile loans, and all of my credit cards would be paid each month." I was incredulous at the foresight of Zobelein at the young age of ten. The outcome of this lifetime strategy has resulted in the mind-blowing list of eight amazing careers, which include the following:

- **Aerospace Industry, Electrical Engineer**—fifteen years. (A component of the Lunar Surveyor Equipment he designed is still located on the moon's surface.)
- **Teacher at the Elementary Level**—fifteen years. (Used computer software to teach academic subjects to children in the classroom.)
- **CEO of a California Corporation**—eleven years. (Made decisions regarding investments in stocks, bonds, and real estate.)
- **Park Ranger in California Regional Park**—ten years. (Led groups through Wildwood Park, which required knowledge of plants and animals as well as the history and culture of the Chumash Indian tribe.)
- **Assistant to a Private Eye**. (Surveillance skills.)
- **Musician and Performer**. (Roles in community theater, playing various instruments, acting, dancing, and singing.)

- **Composer and Producer of a Documentary.** (Producer of CDs and DVDs.)
- **Philanthropist.** (With such nonprofit organizations as New West Symphony and California Lutheran University in Thousand Oaks, California.)

Upon hearing his resume, I became quite awestruck. I asked Zobelein, other than using strategic financial thinking to guide his career, what advice could he give the students? His reply was, "Common sense." With that quick and short response, I wondered if in fact his direction in life had been such a simple one, and as I dug deeper into his life during our interview, I realized that his path was anything but simple and easy. I inquired if he had had any adversity during his life. Zobelein said that during the early part of his life, he had parents who were not supportive of his interests, and they were not well educated, even though they were caring and loved him. He further described his struggles as being a late bloomer in his childhood and being left-handed and dyslexic. His dyslexia was not diagnosed until he was fifty years of age. Another struggle in his life included a poor text memory.

Regardless of all this, Zobelein said, "All of these problematic issues could have hindered me from achieving success; however, I could not and would not let that happen. I persevered with a positive attitude and found ways around these obstacles." Zobelein continued to give advice to the students, which were pearls of wisdom.

Pearls of Wisdom as Told by Craig Zobelein

Zobelein explained during his lecture, "Education in college and in graduate school is very important for understanding theories and developing thinking skills. However, on-the-job training and adaptability to circumstances are critical. In theory, you can analyze how a company should be run, but in the real world, you must provide practical solutions to daily challenges. It is also important to learn the proper use of the English language, and this enabled me to write accurate reports during my career as an electrical engineer. And you need good speaking skills in order to verbalize ideas clearly. Of course, science and math courses provided technical skills in my career as an electrical engineer."

Zobelein continued to discuss the responsibilities of the university and educators. "One of the major responsibilities of universities is to provide the theory to students; however, primarily using theory is not going to be very practical once you graduate. You are going to be inundated with the practice, and you do need the theory behind it, but you also need practical experience. It's one reason I emphasize the need for diverse classes when you are going through college." Zobelein explained that it is important not to get too focused upon the theory in academia, since it is practical experience and common sense that will enable one to succeed in the professional world. He recommended that an individual have a balance between theory from academic studies and practical knowledge that you would gain from the work environment.

Zobelein continued, "What college education did for me was enable me to develop critical thinking skills. My frontal lobe development increased during the time that I spent at the University of Southern California. I have heard it said that you don't fully gain frontal lobe development, which means logical thinking skills, until you are twenty-five years of age. So take that into account.

"It is also important to understand current events. When I was CEO of my family's investment company, I read a lot. I read newspapers, the *Wall Street Journal*, everything relevant, every day, because I wanted to know what was going on in the world and how other companies were accomplishing their goals, which would provide ideas for my own company. Once I got out of college, I believe there were many times where extensive reading was critically important for making decisions. Many times, the material that I read completely changed my perspective on how to have a successful strategy in various situations."

The most important advice that Zobelein gave to the students was the following:

- Whatever your major, don't limit yourself to just that one singular field or course curriculum.
- It is not all about the money but the love of what you are doing and accomplishing in life.

- Find the treasure within you.
- Have an open mind. You may find a different path from the one you originally selected.
- Don't be afraid when opportunity knocks at your mental door. Embrace it!
- Always be able to argue the other person's side to increase negotiation skills.
- Maintain a sense of humor in life and in your professional career, and don't take yourself too seriously. However, don't be so humorous as to lose the respect of your colleagues!

Craig Zobelein in high school

The Education and Early Career of Craig Zobelein

As a young boy, Zobelein pondered what kind of career path he should choose. His initial thought was that he probably would not venture into the area of business since he did not know what the nature of business really was or what skill sets he should have for success. During high school, he became an amateur radio operator, which confirmed his decision to go into the field of electrical engineering. This seemed to be a good fit. He explained, "So engineering seemed like a really natural major for me in college, and it was at a time when the space program was just beginning, and so that had some influence in directing my studies toward that scientific field."

Zobelein decided to study electrical engineering and was accepted in that department at the University of Southern California. He was very proud to be attending college, since he was the first in his family to do so.

At USC, Zobelein mentioned that he had several opportunities to study business courses within the engineering school. He said, "It is ironic that I discovered that business classes provided tremendous value as a student. Also, they required me to take Speech, and I was so frightened at that time about talking in front of people that I was uncomfortable, but by the end, it gave me the confidence to be able to speak in public. After I graduated with an electrical engineering degree from USC, I was able to organize my thoughts and not be afraid to just speak out. I would soon understand that communication skills amongst the people that you work with would be an extremely important and critical aspect not only in the area of engineering but also in my other occupations."

Another revelation that Zobelein would soon understand was the importance of not only being able to communicate effectively on a verbal basis but also in written form. He described his lack of skills in writing. "I was not a good writer in English at all. I wanted to avoid that, and I assumed that having a degree in engineering, there would not be a tremendous need for great skills in writing. I assumed that all I needed to do was worry about calculus, math, and science. Except that when I got out in the real world of engineering, one of the first things I was told after I designed something was that they wanted me to write a manual on how it worked. And it needed to be meticulously detailed, step by step by step—A, B, C, D—and written so anybody out there in the military world or other areas of government would be able to operate this equipment. They said, 'We want you to write this at a sixth-grade level!'"

Zobelein emphasized, "That fascinated me that that was the level at which the public out there was going to use my work. These were mostly military-type products that I was designing. But what happened was that although I had some English skills, I really appreciated the university's desire to have students take English classes, even if they were in a technical field. As I wrote each manual, many times I would submit it to the supervisors, and they tossed it right back to me, saying that it was not written clearly enough, so I would revise the wording."

Zobelein continued to argue his case for the importance of communication skills in the workplace. He cited a specific example from his career as an electrical engineer. "One day I was in my office designing something, and I got a phone call that requested me to please come down to this particular office. So I got up, and when I opened the door, there were about fifty people there, half of them from the United States military and important dignitaries! In my mind, I went, *Uh-oh*. During this period, I was designing a piece of equipment. At the time, I didn't realize it was politically controversial. The customer, being the US military, didn't know whether they really wanted this equipment or not and were not sure that they wanted to pay the money for it.

"So this was kind of like a setup to try to diminish the value of this equipment, so they could make a decision to say, 'No, we are not going to do that.' So off the cuff, and without any rehearsal, I had to verbally describe exactly what I was doing and why that equipment was important. So again, my speaking skills were critical in being able to communicate clearly."

Zobelein said that he came out of the meeting and was slightly stunned by the nature of the events and the controversy surrounding his work. After the meeting was finished, he went to speak to his boss and asked, "So, what was that all about?" "My boss was furious; he had no idea this was going on. Later I learned that they had changed their minds because of my presentation in defense of the equipment. They realized the importance of that particular part of the project, and it was approved. I kept my job!

"During my time as an electrical engineer, I was also required to do proposals to get new business. In a proposal, you not only have to describe how you are going to design the product and what it's going to do but justify the expenditure. So my job was to come up with what the budget was going to be. These costs would consist of design time, engineering time, cost for parts, overhead, and so forth. I had to estimate the budget on a project that hadn't even started yet." Upon hearing Zobelein speak about these budgets that he created, it seemed to be a very complicated and daunting task.

I asked Zobelein, when he created a budget for his projects, did he have a certain return on investment that was required? "Well that's an interesting question, because what would happen is this. I would estimate truthfully what I thought this particular project was going to cost. They didn't give me any parameters. I was to tell them what the budget was going to be. I would do my research and turn the whole proposal into the executives of the company. Then I would get it back, and they would say, 'This is too expensive. Your estimates are not competitive. Find a way to make it less.' Along with other engineers, we would decrease the budget, and ultimately we would ask them, 'Well what figure are you looking for?' They would respond, and finally we would determine what budget would be acceptable so we would be awarded the contract. Then the engineers would have to work overtime at no extra pay in order to complete the project within the budget restraints."

Hughes Lunar Surveyor on moon surface—Craig Zobelein, engineer

Zobelein's Important Engineering Contribution at Hughes and His Transition out of the Field of Engineering

I asked Zobelein about his most important achievements while he was an electrical engineer at Hughes, and he sat back and proudly talked about the work that he and his fellow engineers were able to accomplish. "In 1966, I was very excited to be one of the design engineers for the Surveyor soft landing on the moon, and one of my products is still up there on the surface. It is a brass encoder box that was onboard six Surveyor flights that preceded man landing on the moon. We had to work in a *clean room*, which had a distinctive odor of pure air. I had to wear scrubs, and my hands were always covered with gloves, because we had to be sure that we did not send any contaminants from earth to the moon. We had to put the equipment through rigorous tests and then delicately fix anything that broke. When Surveyor landed successfully, I remember being with all my coworkers at Hughes, Culver City, rejoicing, hugging, and dancing in the hallways. (Of course, I positioned myself next to the cutest secretary!) When I look up at the moon, I am awed to realize that something I held in my hands and helped to design is still up there on the surface!"

To think that he and his team were able to achieve such lofty goals was truly remarkable. I sat there in utter disbelief at the complexity of having a gigantic, complex metallic object be able to be launched into space, make multiple circular orbits, and then have a soft and successful landing on the moon, depositing a piece of equipment that could radio back information to earth. This was indeed an extraordinary and historically important feat for the United States. Zobelein explained that through Hughes he had multiple contracts with the US military and NASA, so indirectly he worked for them as well as Hughes.

While I reflected on the enormity of this task, Zobelein quickly switched gears to the emotional feelings that he began experiencing after working ninety hours per week for a number of years. What I heard from him was that it was a type of burnout from such a highly stressful job. Zobelein began to characterize his thoughts at that period of time. "In my own mind, I was changing goals. So after fifteen years of electrical engineering, I stopped because I was working ninety hours a week, under tremendous pressure, and I realized that I would continue that same workload for a long time. I also sat there realizing I would be in that business, indoors, not seeing the sun about 80 percent of my life! So this sounds like a negative; however, I enjoyed the career I was in very much, but it was time to change. So one day I quit, just like that. I was making a good salary, but it isn't always about the money."

I sat there being incredulous with his bold decision, wondering what in the world he would plan to do for the next professional career in his life. I was also inquisitive as to the nature of how his wife and family would accept his decision to leave such a lucrative post at Hughes. Zobelein also mentioned the heartache that he encountered while at Hughes Aircraft during his last days there as an engineer. He witnessed his boss suffer a mental breakdown, and that also became a catalyst for him to leave. He knew that life was too short to deal with that type of emotional and physical stress for the rest of his working days.

I asked him about having any remorse in moving away from such a lucrative position, and he responded with this advice, "Don't talk about how much money you are going to make or give up as a consequence. That's a sideline to all of this stuff. If you don't enjoy what you are doing, no matter what it is, you can't really feel successful."

Craig Zobelein—Teaching—Career Number Two

I would soon hear, much to my anticipation, the career path that Zobelein pursued next. He admitted that once he quit his engineering job, he had no idea what his professional career would be, but he was not worried. He spent the whole summer puttering around in the garden, which was therapeutic. This reminded me of the statement that he previously made, which involved having no debt by forty-five years of age and being able to pursue whatever career paths that he wanted to without any financial concerns.

He continued, "I had a great deal of self-confidence. I knew that the world is exciting, and I was ready for the next project, and I've always been curious about teaching, and my wife, Jennifer, was also interested in teaching at that time. So we looked at each other and said, 'Let's go back and get teaching credentials.' So we enrolled at a wonderful school nearby, California Lutheran University. I remember I just jumped into it by taking nine units in the summer. What a phenomenal experience it was—to be able to open up, learn, and have an opportunity to go back to school in a totally different field. So anyway, it took two years to complete the thirty units, plus student teaching. Believe it or not, I wanted to focus on education at the elementary level. I went from state-of-the-art engineering to teaching in an elementary school classroom!

I asked Zobelein what years he attended California Lutheran University, and he said it was 1979–80. He commented that he was truly proud of being a straight-A student at the university (unlike his years at USC), and this did not come as a surprise to me, knowing that he had developed critical thinking skills. Zobelein relished the time that he spent at CLU getting his teaching credential, and he said that it was one of the most rewarding times of his life.

He spoke about his early teaching career at the elementary school level. "I really learned a lot in my teaching career. Again, it got back to verbal communication, and it also involved a great deal of mental preparation and organization. One of the things about teaching, as in any kind of a business, is that you have to organize your day. You have to say, step one, step two, step three, because particularly with antsy young children, you have to keep them challenged. You have to keep them going and motivate them, and you can't escape and go and sit in an office. So my challenge in that particular career was to be able to organize my thoughts and plans for each day and keep thirty active little children busy and physically and mentally occupied."

Zobelein continued to draw the comparison between teaching and operating a business. "I also think that is true when you are managing a business. In business, there may not be little antsy children, but believe me, there are still antsy grown adults, and they still have their issues and their problems both at home and at work. Many are wondering, *Am I doing what I need to do? Does the boss still like me?* There are a lot of things to organize, strategize, and supervise as the boss or owner of a business. My teaching career really helped in multiple ways. So up until that time, I had two careers, fifteen years of engineering, followed by fifteen years of teaching."

I thought that was a very interesting coincidence, to have two careers of fifteen years each. Zobelein said, "So at the end of fifteen years of teaching, I thought it was time to make another change. It's really important to not stubbornly stick with what you think you want to do. Keep an open mind about it. Look for opportunity. Watch, look, and listen, and by listen, I mean listen to your inner thoughts and listen to what other people are saying to you. That can be critically important to how you are going to conduct yourself through one career or through many careers. It doesn't matter how many careers you have; it only matters that you live life to the fullest and with passion!"

Craig Zobelein—CEO, Family Business—Career Number Three

At the time that Zobelein quit teaching, his family owned a business, the Zobelein Company, based on financial and real estate investments. He described his next move from being a teacher to becoming the CEO of his family's business in 1993. Zobelein talked about this transition from career number two to career three. "My wife had business and accounting skills, and she also was an English major and an author. So we reviewed each other's careers and realized that with these skills, we could make a strong team and greatly contribute to the needs of my family's business. We would pursue executive positions, and I would apply for the position of CEO of the family corporation, Zobelein Company, and my wife would apply as an office manager."

Zobelein continued, "So even though it was family, we still had to be interviewed, submit full resumes, and they put us through the mill to see whether or not we were qualified for these positions. Fortunately, we were hired. Now you might ask how in the world did that new job have anything to do with either engineering or teaching? It has to do with common sense and logical thinking skills. You just have to analyze any business you go into, consider what needs to be done and how you can achieve those goals."

I was truly fascinated to hear of the examples that Zobelein used to logically explain these multiple careers. Although these careers were very

A Village of Knowledge

diverse, he utilized a core principle. "When I first took over the company, I really didn't know much about it. My family had not shared with me at all what was really going on with this business. I had to make certain assumptions about the business in order for my resume to match the credentials of what they were looking for in a CEO. Fortunately, these assumptions turned out to be rather accurate. So day one, I am sitting at my desk in the office on Olympic Boulevard in Los Angeles, and I am reviewing what the company does. While looking at the company's statements, I realized I had to read a great deal more in the area of business law and finance."

I continued to be amazed at the agility of this man, to be able to handle so many different career responsibilities, and I wondered if this job as CEO for his family had anything to do with money or his salary. Zobelein responded, "It had nothing to do with money. I was not there for the money. I was there to run a business and to do it better than my predecessors. Soon I discovered that Zobelein Company had been spending $30,000 a year in rent for their office space, but I also observed that the company owned apartments in downtown LA, only fifteen or twenty minutes from its office location. Of the forty-eight units, half of them were empty, partly due to racial unrest (Watts riots) in that area of the city at that time. So, I said, "Why are we spending $30,000 a year when our business can use one of those free apartments for office space?" So immediately, I gave notice to the lessor, and after two months, we moved into the apartment building we owned. So I was saving the stockholders $30,000 a year. In the 1990s, that was a fair amount of money. So that was my first business decision for the company. Following that, I authorized some major improvements to the property that made it more secure and appealing to potential residents. Immediately, we attracted more renters (since we were in close proximity to both USC and the Coliseum), and it wasn't long until all the units were full."

Zobelein continued to use logic for implementing his business strategies. "I looked over the portfolio of the company investments and noticed that it consisted primarily of common stocks, which looked fine to me, and they were making good returns." But he recognized that the company's investments lacked diversification, and he noted that there were no bonds in the portfolio. Zobelein said that at that time bond yields were close to 5–6 percent, with much higher yields than in today's market.

Zobelein explained, "Some of these bonds of course were tax-free both at the state and federal level. So I asked one of the older family members, 'Why are there no bonds in the company's portfolio?' I was told that fifty years ago, the company had a large amount invested in bonds, which at that time brought a very low return. It turned out to be a very poor investment, and all of the invested capital was lost." He said that those family members who were financiers in the company had intentionally stayed away from buying bonds from their previous experience over fifty years ago. Zobelein reversed that decision and began investing in municipal bonds with a good return. He implied, in a slightly humble manner, that he thought the family members who were previously managing the company might have had some concerns about his investment philosophy, but they allowed him to proceed. "I served the Zobelein Company for eleven years as the CEO, and in the first five years, I doubled the stockholders' income. How did I do that? Common sense, looking at everything and saying, what's wrong, what can I do to fix it, and keeping an open mind about business strategy."

Again, I continued to be impressed by the diversity not only of his portfolio skills as the CEO of the company but also the success he had with each of his very diverse careers.

Zobelein—Dispute Resolution Arbitrator as CEO

Zobelein described another issue regarding the business strategy as CEO of the company that involved an eminent domain dispute between his family's property and Caltrans Downtown LA. "Caltrans was expanding the 110 freeway and needed some of our property adjoining the freeway, which included one of our apartment buildings plus a portion of the parking lot. We had a lawyer, and when I took over, I noticed that the company was paying him $3,000 a quarter, but no progress was being made. The lawyer would send a letter to Caltrans saying what the family wanted, and Caltrans would come back with its demands. The letters would constantly go back and forth without any resolution for this eminent domain dispute. So when I came in as CEO, I said, this is ridiculous, I am going to handle this myself. I went to the lawyer and said, 'I am going to arrange a meeting with the Caltrans people in their downtown office and get this settled.' So our lawyer said, 'Fine, just let me know what you are going to do and what you decide.' I agreed. I didn't want to completely bypass my lawyer."

Zobelein described the scene as he arrived in the Caltrans conference room. "I get down there and open the door, and there must have been fifty people or so in this room, all Caltrans executives, and me. When I went in there, I realized that what I needed to do first was listen to them and their arguments that were being presented. After a half hour or so of listening to what their problems were with this eminent domain issue that we were involved in, I realized that they had very little cash from the state of California, but they had many skilled laborers who were available! As I listened to their side of the argument, mentally I was developing my company's strategy. *How can I dovetail our business needs with their business needs, rather than what we can take from the state of California and get as much money as we can?* In other words, what could we all agree on that would be of mutual benefit?"

As I heard Zobelein describe the circumstances of the Caltrans meeting, it was crystal clear that he was using his listening, arbitration, and communication skills to cut a clear path to resolving the issue. There was much empathy on his part also since, as was mentioned before, he always tried to understand the perspective of the party opposing him, in order to make a better argument for his viewpoint.

He continued to describe his persuasive skills of negotiation during the meeting, "So I started fitting the pieces of the puzzle together, and I realized that we had a one-story, two-unit apartment building on the property, which was not even being rented, with an attached parking area." I wondered why the apartments were not being rented, and he responded that they were filled with the toxic substance asbestos. Obviously, he and his company did not want to risk any lawsuits with this dangerous substance that could jeopardize a tenant's health and therefore kept those units vacant. Nor did his family's company want to deal with the removal of the hazardous material, which would be very expensive. So they just used it for storage. I continued to listen to his resolution.

"So I looked at the Caltrans delegation, and I inquired if it would possible that they could demolish those two apartment units which contained asbestos? In exchange, they would be given a portion of the parking lot adjoining the freeway for their construction of a new off-ramp. The Caltrans delegation responded and said, 'Oh yes, we can do that!' So their HAZMAT employees who specialize in the removal of hazardous materials came in with their asbestos outfits on, and they tore those buildings down. They also repaved the underlying ground for additional tenant parking."

So as I listened to Zobelein, it was clear that this resolution had been one of the most rewarding experiences in negotiations that he had during his career as CEO in his family's business. Obviously he had handled this dispute in a more astute and clever way than their lawyer who had only been sending letters in the mail for months on end and had accomplished nothing.

He continued to emphasize the importance of critical thinking during this experience. Apparently, that was not the only positive outcome from this meeting with Caltrans. Zobelein explained, "Two months later, I got a phone call from Caltrans, and they said they had really enjoyed working with me." They explained that they appreciated his win-win strategy. Zobelein's viewpoint wasn't based on what his family company could take but rather on the possible give and take between both sides. Much to the amazement of Zobelein, Caltrans continued by saying, "'We actually wound up with some extra land right next to yours that we are not going to use. You can have it for free.' That was unprecedented, and of course we accepted it for additional tenant parking. And that pretty much covers my career as CEO of my family's business."

I was completely impressed by Zobelein's aptitude for business strategy, creative thinking, and dispute resolution. With that impressive record, and after eleven years as the CEO of Zobelein Company, he decided again that it was time to move on to yet another career!

A Village of Knowledge

Craig Zobelein as park ranger

Craig Zobelein—Park Ranger—Career Four

As Zobelein described his following career, he continued to emphasize that even though they were all very diverse, they all required good speech, communication, and creative skills. He began to describe yet another career, and I continue to be astonished at the breadth of his professional diversity. "I was a park ranger for Wildwood Regional Park for ten years, and I received a state award because I did a good job. Why did I do a good job? It was because I had a diverse set of skills. I gave campfire programs and hikes, and I wrote material describing the flora and fauna of Wildwood Park. That was fun, and it was exciting, since I got to work with Wildwood Park visitors and inform them about the area. Sometimes they would come to me and inquire, 'What did the Chumash Indians eat during the time that they lived in this area?' I would give a talk, and we would go out in the field, and we would eat what they ate." Zobelein also described that the Indians would use all of the materials that they hunted, which included the food being eaten and the fur from the deer, which was worn during cold weather.

Zobelein again described the value of the classes he took while he was at USC and at California Lutheran University, and how he was able to use the subjects from academia and put them to practical use in his multiple careers. He explained, "I built on that because you know that what you learn in the classroom is only to give you an indication of what you can do with those various courses. You can amplify that in so many exciting and different ways once you get out."

Craig Zobelein—Private Detective— Career Number Five

As Zobelein discussed his next professional career, he spoke about his entry into the life of a private detective. He said that this career was brief, and he only spent several years in this profession. I inquired how he became interested in this field of what I would call the world of spying or espionage. "It began with my neighbor knocking at my door. The man said, 'You know that I am a private detective, and I know that you have an engineering background. Well, I am tired of doing surveillance in my car in 110 degrees, sitting there for eight hours.' He asked me if I could install a video camera in his car that would record a scene for an entire day. He wanted to be able to do this from his car while he could go away and come back later to look at the tape and see what had transpired."

Zobelein told his neighbor that he would be able to do that, but the equipment at that time in the 1980s was cumbersome and difficult to set up quickly. However, he figured it out and for about a year or two helped his neighbor with surveillance related to insurance fraud cases. He said, "So we were able to catch the bad guys with that particular project, and that was a lot of fun and very satisfying."

Zobelein—Life Lessons from Many Generations and How This Influenced His Life

I became very inquisitive about the nature of his family history, and indeed he had a very interesting story to tell about his family and their business, which started in the early 1900s. I believed that there might be some genetic link to all of the contributions that he had made, his tenacity, and his overall insatiable curiosity, and I predicted that it had a lot to do with his ancestors.

Zobelein explained the history of his family in California, and he mentioned that he was the fourth generation from Los Angeles. "Our company started in the early 1900s. My great-grandfather came from Germany. He was tired of fighting in the Prussian war, so he immigrated through Ellis Island and ended up on the West Coast during the gold rush days of California. My great-grandfather thought, *I'm not going to break my back or waste my time panning for gold. Instead, I will sell supplies to the miners*. So he started a general store in the town of Panamint in central California and sold mining equipment and other things. That was smart! Later on, he moved to Los Angeles.

"At any rate, he saved his money and ended up marrying a woman who owned a grant for a large parcel of land in downtown Los Angeles, near where USC and the Coliseum are now located. He developed that land and made a profit, and then he started a brewery, which was the beginning of the family business." Zobelein described that this was the first brewery on the West Coast of the United States, the Los Angeles Brewing Company. Later on, during prohibition, the brewery sold Near Beer with an allowable low alcoholic content. It was marketed as being good for sciatica and safe for pregnant women. Here is an example of working around a barrier. "Rather than my great-grandfather just quitting and going out of business, he found a way to continue." To mark the end of prohibition, they had Jean Harlow, a renowned actress at that time, break a bottle of beer over their lead delivery truck. The trucks were filled with real beer, and they started to roll again, delivering all over Southern California. This scene received a lot of press and publicity in Hollywood.

Again, one could make the argument that a large part of the DNA or genetic makeup of Craig Zobelein came from his great-grandfather who had great tenacity and a tremendously positive attitude in business and in life. Zobelein mentioned also that he was of German descent, with a very stubborn, determined character, and against all odds, he was determined to succeed. These were typical German personality attributes.

I asked Zobelein to tell me more about his great-grandfather. He continued by describing him as having stern good looks, and he was a man you would not mess around with. Zobelein said, "Being of German descent, it was ironic that he married a woman from Mexico." I immediately thought that was where Craig got the creative side of his personality, from his great-grandmother. Zobelein's love for dance and music probably came from that side of his family. Zobelein responded, "In fact, I did grow up with that influence. My aunts loved Mexican and Spanish folkloric dancing, and I remember growing up as a child they would have fiestas in their courtyards, and they would all have these big, flowing Mexican dresses, and of course the beer from our family's brewery was also flowing!"

Zobelein said that as an older child and a young adult, his parents would allow him to drink, but he made the conscious decision that he would only taste the beer and not partake or drink it. So he was a taster and not a drinker! Zobelein, as he attended these family parties, came to the conclusion that alcoholic beverages could do more harm than good. "This stuff can harm you, but I can't say that I'm a teetotaler since I taste; however, I am not a drinker. I never drank in my life. I tasted. That's more what I did." We spoke more about tasting, and I said that perhaps with tasting, one could make the correlation with his motivation, passion, and inspiration to taste life. To taste life and all that it has to offer would be one of Craig Zobelein's more interesting legacies.

I then inquired about his parents and their behavior in terms of alcoholic beverages. "My father drank socially but responsibly. My mother, on the other hand, was a different story. She would be classified today as an alcoholic, and there were times when I would come home and have to peel her off the kitchen floor. So it was another interesting thing of my childhood to have to deal with." I responded by saying that this must have shaped his life as well, seeing his mother go through those trials and tribulations. Zobelein later said that his mother, even though she smoked and drank, died at the ripe old age of eighty-three from emphysema.

This led to our next conversation about the outcome of the family beer beverage business. The business was called the LA Brewing Company, and they manufactured two products, Eastside Beer and Old Mission Beer. Zobelein, a fourth-generation Los Angeles resident, said that their beer business was largely successful and was sold to Pabst Blue Ribbon for millions of dollars in 1948. The profits were utilized for developing the land they owned and also invested in stocks and bonds.

Zobelein, as the CEO of the company, said that with each generation, the shares became divided to such an extent that they eventually liquidated the Zobelein Company in 2011, each family stockholder receiving his or her proportionate amount in cash.

Craig Zobelein on the ham radio

The Strong Influence of Zobelein's Father

Zobelein began by talking in more depth about his father and their relationship as he was growing up. He said that his father had a big impact on him, even though he said that their relationship was not very close. "My father had a big influence on me. He was a stockbroker, and I watched what he did with his investments and listened to his political views about the government spending too much money." Zobelein also said that even though his father worked all the time as a stockbroker, it seemed that they didn't have much in terms of wealth. I remembered that he previously said that at age ten, Zobelein realized that he wanted to be able to retire at age forty-five and be debt-free, without a mortgage or credit card debt. He said, "All of the financial strife that my father went through began to sink into me, even at ten years old. I observed that people were working all of the time—nine, ten, twelve hours a day—and they were turning that money over to a first mortgage bank to pay off their home loans. I understood on an intuitive level that the bank was making all of the money. I said that's ridiculous. So, I decided at ten years old I was going to have a goal to have no debts by the time I was forty-five years old, including a first mortgage."

I asked Zobelein if he had a personal conversation with his father about the meaning of debt and risk at the tender age of ten. He replied, "That's an interesting question. I never really talked to him in that way; as much as he was a good father and he influenced me, we couldn't talk to one another really well." He felt that his father did have a great influence on him in regard to his own personal financial management. His father taught him the importance of working hard, saving your money, investing wisely, and managing risk throughout one's life.

Growing up, Zobelein felt pretty much on his own. However, he became more communicative with the encouragement of his mother. Zobelein did feel isolated as he grew up into a young man. "Most of what I did in my life, unfortunately, my parents did not help me. However, this statement is not made to disrespect my parents, since they did have a great deal of influence on me, but I made my own decisions."

I asked him if he ever thought about inheriting anything from his parents, and he said that he did not worry, nor did he expect an inheritance throughout his life. This philosophy had much to do with the financial lessons that his father taught him about being independent. Apparently this philosophy became of great value to Zobelein, since he was able to retire from Hughes Aircraft at forty-five years of age, and due to no debt was able to move on into other careers. "Coincidentally, as it happened, at the time I made my last mortgage payment, I quit my engineering employment at Hughes Aircraft." I responded with the thought that he had the insight at ten years old to not be burdened by debt and had thirty-five years to get his nest egg together, so then he went back to school, became a teacher, CEO of a family corporation, park ranger, and an assistant to a private eye, and went into several other important careers. This was all done after the age of forty-five, when he was not dependent on a certain salary for his overhead.

He was also able to accomplish the goals with the support of his wife, Jennifer. Both being very practical people in regard to money and finances, they agreed that they should wait and have children seven years into their marriage. They worked hard, saved their money, and were able to pay their cars off and pay down the mortgage principal on their house. Zobelein explained that they did not drive fancy cars or have an exotic lifestyle.

Our conversation then led to his decision to become an engineer. Zobelein explained that his father had a big influence on these career goals as well. His father bought him a shortwave receiver and made him a crystal set. Zobelein said, "I had been a ham radio operator during my early teenage years and went on the air quite a bit and enjoyed doing that. I would go on the air late at night and listen to people talking to one another across the world. This was fascinating. Again, that fit into my curious mind." He said that was in the 1950s during the Cold War with Russia.

He explained, "Shortwave also involved listening to other ham radio operators from Burma and from places around the world, Japan and all over, and many of them spoke English. English was becoming a more universal language, and therefore, we as amateur radio operators could speak to each other in English. I guess you could call it eavesdropping. Professionals would use it for spying. Of course, you could also pick up radio stations from around the world. I'd hear music from Asian countries and European countries. I would be up until three and four in the morning listening to these radio station conversations as a young teenager." Zobelein emphasized the fact that this drove his curiosity, which led him to become interested in engineering and space exploration. So this radio device, a gift from his father, played a big role in his pursuit of an engineering degree.

Even though his father did not obtain a college degree, his father was very smart and was even able to tutor young Craig through geometry proofs in high school. Zobelein explained that his grades through school were only mediocre. He was a C student. However, what he lacked in high grades he made up for with curiosity, drive, and an emotional quotient. "Despite the mediocre grades, I was a success in all of my careers. I left contributions behind in each one."

He said that his confidence and ambition were much higher than those of his father. "I refused to let a C grade interfere with my knowledge of things. I have an innate curiosity about life, about learning new things, and a C grade is not going to stop me from learning." I recognized that as Zobelein spoke, he was always working hard to push himself forward. He did not have any fear of failure. He also had a tremendously positive attitude in life.

Left to right: Craig Zobelein dancing: flamenco, ball room, and jazz

Craig Zobelein—Careers Six, Seven, Eight—Performing, Dancing, Composing, Philanthropy, and Life Lessons

I continued to be impressed as he described his further involvement in dancing, music, composing, and philanthropy. I was curious how someone could be advanced on both sides of the brain—from the left side of the brain, which focuses on logic and technical skills, and the right side of the brain, which is more prone to artistic goals and creativity. He explained, "In fact this is another interesting question, 'Are you right brained or left brained?' That's an important feature of what you are going to do in your career. I have always said that I have a clash between my right brain and my left brain because all of the biographical information I told you about so far has of course been left-brained activity: logic, thinking skills, and the more academic approach. However, I also have a right brain that is very active. My mother was in show business and was an opera singer in the 1930s and 1940s, so I have an influence in that direction. My mother said, 'I don't want you going into show business. I want you to have a family and a steady job.' So I took her advice and focused on the left side of my brain, in engineering."

After he retired, he was able to open up his more creative side and pursue his love of the arts. Zobelein began to pursue his first creative passion with dance. He described that he was a principal dancer for six years in a ballet company, doing *The Nutcracker* multiple times. He said, "So I got to twirl the girls and lift them in the air. That's what I found out the man does. Every now and then, they let me leap through the air. It was an interesting activity, to say the least." In regard to *The Nutcracker* ballet, Zobelein said he did so many of those performances that he never wanted to see *The Nutcracker* ballet again! Zobelein's experience in dancing did not stop with ballet. He described his two years of involvement as a flamenco dancer. He had a female partner and a live guitarist, and the three of them would go around and do shows at various places.

Zobelein grew up in a home filled with music. His mother was an opera star, and his father frequently played recordings of classical favorites. Eventually, he learned to play the banjo, guitar, accordion, and harmonica. Often as a child, he would go to the piano, playing and making up simple songs on the keyboard.

This led him in his adult life to revisit the piano, and he became serious about playing and composing his own songs. He had little intention of doing that professionally until one day he had a conversation with Bob Bockholt, the music librarian and stage manager for the New West Symphony, a professional orchestra in Thousand Oaks, California. Bockholt had previously worked as an arranger for Arthur Fiedler and the Boston Pops. Upon hearing Zobelein's original musical works, Bockholt was impressed and said that he would like to arrange his music for the orchestra, if he wished. Of course Zobelein said yes!

Virginia Gean, MBA, CMA

Craig Zobelein on the Walt Disney Concert Hall organ and on the Roland Atelier

He then began to compose and perform and currently has two CDs out on iTunes, Amazon.com, and CD Baby. One of them is called *Big Band Stew* and includes six of his compositions, played by a twenty-two-piece band. The other CD is called *Music Is Magic (Live)* and features him playing a variety of popular songs on the Roland Atelier, plus a little singing, too. Subsequently, he was commissioned by New West Symphony to compose a fanfare to celebrate its twentieth anniversary. This was performed onstage and included a ninety-person choir singing the words he also provided along with the orchestral score. One of his proudest achievements was coproducing with his wife a documentary entitled *The Walt Disney Concert Hall Organ* (packaged as a DVD with bonus CD), which describes the design and construction of this iconic Los Angeles pipe organ through a lovely interweaving of facts with musical excerpts. All of these projects required a great deal of creativity as well as business skills.

As Zobelein became more involved with his musical career, both he and his wife made a conscious decision to be philanthropists of the New West Symphony. They became great benefactors of the organization and helped the symphony during a time of financial distress. They were also very generous donors to California Lutheran University, helping the music department by providing much-needed funds for orchestral instruments and a practice organ as well as scholarships for students.

Craig Zobelein, 2016

The Importance of the Crossover of Creativity into Business

Zobelein emphasized the importance of using creativity in business. As he said, "You know the creative brain is also very beneficial to business. It's that part of you that allows you to create something new and interesting, not just follow a textbook or follow what somebody thinks you should do. Use these creative ideas and implement them into your business strategy." He explained that one should let the mind flow between the left and right parts of the brain, and that the most successful businesses are deeply based in creativity. As he described this philosophy, my immediate thoughts came to rest on the tremendous creativity of Steve Jobs with Apple computer and the magnificent blend of his creativity, innovation, and business acumen, which ultimately produced a multibillion-dollar business.

"In each career I have pursued, it's been very exciting to let my mind flow like that, and even if you stick with one particular career, you can still let the creativity flow. Also giving to others is what it is really all about, giving to people and sharing what you have learned. I think that each person has a treasure within. They need to find this talent and develop it."

Zobelein spoke about his life philosophy. "I am convinced through the treasures that I have discovered within me in all these different careers that everybody has more than one treasure, but many times they don't look for it. They don't even realize they have a treasure within them that's hidden somewhere. So I really think it's important to be able to question yourself and to look deep inside you and gain that excitement about something new and let that treasure come out. Don't bury it within you or think you can't do anything else."

Zobelein continued, "My attitude has always been, all right, everybody in life has a barrier. My view is: don't stop at the barrier. Find a way to get over it or around it, and that's the challenge, isn't it? Not to be discouraged by the obstacles. The challenge is finding out how to overcome that barrier. You may not know what it is. You may have to try this and try that, but don't be afraid to try."

As we ended our interview with Mr. Craig Zobelein, I believed that I was hearing and witnessing a true Renaissance man, with his multiple careers, talents, and wisdom that he wanted to pass on to other generations through his extraordinary life.

Chapter 6

Jennifer Zobelein-Author: *A Forest of Pipes*-Story of Disney Organ, Philanthropist and Teacher

Jennifer Zobelein

Author of *A Forest Of Pipes, the Story of the Walt Disney Concert Hall Organ*; Co-Executive Producer of the Documentary *The Walt Disney Concert Hall Organ*; Philanthropist; Former President of New West Symphony; Supporter of Many Nonprofits.

**Giving and Serving Others Creates Great Joy in Life
The Importance of Communication**

As Jennifer Zobelein enters the room to be interviewed, she appears with a beautiful bright smile, briefcase, and a personality that reflects complete grace, poise, and confidence. She comes to our meeting totally prepared for our interview and soon begins to describe her journey from her childhood in England during World War II through adulthood. It soon becomes apparent that Zobelein, with her wide range of talent, careers, and education, is a very special human being who bestows much knowledge without being boastful. She, as many other leaders in this book, has a spirit that is both humble and generous.

Photos from World War II in the war-torn nation of England

Early Childhood in War-Torn Britain and the Move to the United States

Zobelein begins to tell her story by describing her upbringing as a child. She was born in England during the time of the bombing raids over the war-torn nation in World War II. She had many experiences in air-raid shelters and considered it a time of danger and excitement. In fact, as a child, her house in England was bombed, although she and her family were not present at that time. They returned and made repairs and continued to live there. One recurring theme during her interviews was to never take anything in life for granted and to always be the best you can be, in both your personal and professional lives. Zobelein would continue throughout her life to pursue the appropriate education and skills needed to be a high achiever in whatever fields she sought. Indeed, to read the resume of Zobelein, it becomes apparent that she has succeeded professionally in many areas in multiple careers.

After surviving the bombing raids in World War II in England, she and her family moved to Toronto, Canada, to seek a better life away from the shattered European nation. After spending a few years living in Toronto, they moved on to Vancouver, British Columbia. As a high school student, she and her family made another move to Southern California in 1955.

This immigration to the United States provided additional opportunities for her as a young adult. Moving to America was the dream of millions of individuals who perceived the United States as a shining beacon for supreme opportunity, for freedom, prosperity, peace, and the ability to pursue happiness.

Young Adulthood—High School and UCLA

After her move to Southern California, Zobelein enrolled in high school in Los Angeles. She had one of the top academic records in her senior year, and she was invited to be one of the commencement speakers at her graduation. Even in high school, Zobelein understood the importance of a strong liberal arts education. Her graduation commencement speech was very well received. A parent of one of her friends suggested she should go to law school. However, she had an intuition that she would prefer to write, teach, communicate, and interact, with students with a potential career in teaching upon graduating from college. Although she would have enjoyed law school, she chose a different path.

During her senior year of high school, Zobelein applied to UCLA, where she was admitted as a student with a planned major in English and a minor in music. However, prior to full enrollment in UCLA as a freshman, Zobelein decided to take a year of business courses at Santa Monica City College in order to have practical job skills. She took classes in accounting, business law, economics, typing, shorthand, and office management. She understood the wisdom of having diverse skills prior to attending UCLA as a freshman. Zobelein, being ever so practical, took her studies in these areas very seriously and was able to secure summer employment each year, which enabled her to earn her tuition for UCLA. She commented, "A person might end up with an undergraduate degree in philosophy and come out with graduation cap and gown on, and at the end of the day realize that there was nothing suitable for a job or a career. So perhaps it is wiser to study in those areas which are less theoretical and provide a greater opportunity for employment."

After her year of studying business at Santa Monica City College, Zobelein enrolled at UCLA. Her four years of education there proved to be very valuable in the field of liberal arts, with a BA in English and a minor in music. Later in life, she served as a church organist in Ventura County and as dean of the local chapter of the American Guild of Organists for three years. Her love of music and playing the organ served her well during the latter part of her career.

Zobelein expands on one of the leading principles for learning that she was taught in college, which was the study of Bloom's taxonomy. Bloom's taxonomy is a list of learning objectives that was introduced by Benjamin Bloom in the 1950s and is shared by a large number of educators. The list describes a set of six levels of thinking and lists them according to importance from the least important at the bottom to the most important at the top. Ironically, at the bottom of the list is knowledge. For clarification purposes, the diagram below illustrates how Bloom's taxonomy is defined, beginning with knowledge as only the beginning of the thinking process.

Bloom's Taxonomy Conceptual Framework–The Importance of Critical Thinking in Education

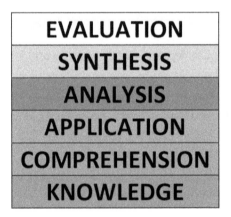

Bloom's taxonomy

Zobelein explained the importance of this Bloom's taxonomy model during her education at UCLA. "You would normally think that you go to college because you want to gain knowledge, but that's only the beginning. I mean, that's the foundation. A parrot can spout off knowledge, but the next level is comprehension. Do you really understand what that knowledge means? And then the next level is application. Can you take that knowledge and apply it to something and do something useful with it? And then even higher up the scale is analysis. Can you think through what this really means and what the significance of it would be? And then higher than that is synthesis. Can you take all of that knowledge and comprehension and put it together into something new, something creative, synthesize it into perhaps a new project? At the top of the pyramid is evaluation. Can you then look at what has been accomplished and truly judge and evaluate how worthwhile that has been? To my mind, that is what college students need because those are the critical thinking skills that prepare you for the world, because you don't know where life will lead you. But if you can be a good thinker, then you can be successful, and that can be applied to so many different areas of life." Zobelein continued to emphasize that these concepts should be learned in school and practiced throughout one's career.

Jennifer Zobelein in Her Young Adult Career

After graduating from UCLA in 1962, with a bachelor of arts in English and a minor in music, she worked as an assistant editor for Western Publishing Company in Los Angeles, where she wrote fiction, nonfiction, educational materials, advertising copy, and record inserts. She also did editing and proofreading. Western Publishing produced the Little Golden Books, Gold Key comics, puzzles, games, playing cards, children's records, cookbooks, and encyclopedias. (On her own time, she agreed to write political speeches for a friend who was running for Congress.)

Listening to her during her interview, it became apparent that one of Zobelein's favorite responsibilities while working at the Western Publishing Company was her involvement with their comic books. She commented that these comic books, in the 1950s and 1960s, were wholesome, adhering to a strict code then in place in the industry. Zobelein fondly recalls writing educational nonfiction text pages for inclusion in such comic books as *Korak, Son of Tarzan, Space Family Robinson, The Jetsons, Duke* of the *K-9 Patrol*, and *Magnus, Robot Fighter*. Her subjects covered such things as what astronauts eat in space, rocketry and missiles, energy for the future, space travel, radio telescopes, plants and animals of Africa, and the domestication of dogs.

One of her most interesting projects was a pop-up book that she wrote for Hallmark entitled *Great Dinosaurs*. The paper mechanics were created by an artist, but she provided the written descriptions of six well-known dinosaurs. She truly enjoyed researching the subject matter, reading over twenty nonfiction books on the subject to provide the accurate content. Zobelein explained that the *Great Dinosaurs* book became quite a hit and sold many copies. Hallmark would later sell it to Troll Books. Troll Books published its updated edition but did not list her name on the cover of the book as being the writer because she had received a flat fee for the original edition and therefore had no rights to any royalties or credits for either edition. Nevertheless, she knew that she was the author of this—her first published book.

Left to right: Jennifer Zobelein high school graduation and Jennifer Zobelein as a teacher

The Importance of Communication, Writing, Education, and Teaching

Over the years, both she and her husband decided on a new professional career in teaching. Together they decided to pursue their teaching

A Village of Knowledge

credentials at California Lutheran University, each earning a bachelor of arts in education. Their two children were still pre-high school students.

Zobelein reflects, "Throughout my life, I have gained experience in writing, in teaching, and in producing various creative projects. I think students who are in college often wonder, *Where will this degree take me?* Quite often, we end up in different places that we could not have foreseen. So, I just jotted down a few notes here. The study of language that I pursued at UCLA and later at California Lutheran University, I think, is so important because communication skills are vital, whether it's verbal or written communication. Those skills apply to so many areas of life that it's important that students know how to express themselves clearly. So when I was in school, I had no idea that this is where my degree would lead me, but how satisfying that has been because I think part of it, too, is being curious. I've just always had an unstoppable curiosity." Over the next fifteen years, Zobelein taught at the kindergarten, elementary, secondary, junior high, and high school levels. In teaching, she had a tremendous desire to encourage students to write and communicate well. She had a strong passion to engage her students and to emphasize the true importance of creative thinking. Zobelein said that this passion to educate students to write and think critically would reach across all age groups, from elementary to adult.

Zobelein expressed the sheer joy of teaching very gifted students in the elementary education program in Simi Valley. "I was teaching in a program for gifted students. These were elementary students who were pulled out, and they came to me one day a week, and this was really good for them because they were accustomed to being the only gifted student in the classroom. Suddenly, they were pulled out into a classroom where everyone had a high IQ and were good thinkers. It was more competitive for them. It was great. Actually, I had three students who were deaf, and they came with an interpreter."

She continued, "This was good for the other gifted students to see because people tend to think, *Oh well, if you're deaf, you're also dumb*, which of course is not true. So for them to see that you could be deaf but also gifted was a great learning experience for them. Then at the end of the year, I set up an obstacle course in the playground, and all of the students, both the deaf students and the students with no disabilities, had to go through in groups of two or three, and they were blindfolded one at a time, and the other one or two in their group had to figure out a way to communicate to them how to get through the obstacle course without speaking. Well, for the deaf students, they were not only blind but they were also deaf, and they couldn't do it by talking; they had to come up with some method of communication, whether it was tapping a pencil on a can with a little code or whatever they chose to tell this other student how to get through the course. Well, the deaf students went through zip-a-dee-doo—faster than anybody."

I responded incredulously, inquiring how that was possible. But then I realized that it was very logical, based on the deaf students developing their senses in more ways than the other students would normally do. Zobelein answered, "These deaf students were used to coping with difficulties and found ways to be creative in order to deal with their disabilities. So whereas some of the other gifted students had really complicated codes and signals and all this to get them through the course, the deaf students kept it very simple. It was just a little tap on the shoulder: one, two, three—three steps forward; one, two—two steps to the right; one—one step to the left, and they got right through."

I asked her if she came up with the maze idea, and she responded yes! Again I was incredibly impressed with the level of critical thinking that Zobelein used in teaching these students. I was reminded of her studies at UCLA with Bloom's taxonomy and her knowledge and usage of critical thinking in the classroom. This teaching was indeed creative and tapped into the theory of Bloom's taxonomy from the lower base of knowledge, comprehension, application, and climbing upward on this theory of analysis, to synthesis, up to evaluation. As I listened to Zobelein during the interview, it was evident that her skills as a teacher and a leader were remarkable!

I inquired, which of her students finished the maze first? She said, "Well, we went back in the classroom and discussed it, and we found that the deaf students finished first. They were the most efficient, and three of my brightest gifted students who were working together, who had egos (because a lot of gifted students do), never could agree on what they would use as a method to get themselves through that obstacle course, and so they didn't even go through it. That was such a lesson for everybody in the classroom to see, and it was a very educational experience for all of us. That is a wonderful example of the importance of communication skills!"

Zobelein continued, "So then we had a big discussion about, well, okay, you may be really gifted, whether it's in math or science or performing arts, or whatever, but if you're so gifted that you have to end up just being in a think tank and not communicating with anybody in the real world because you don't know how to convey those ideas in a way that's useful, what's the good of being gifted? If you can't communicate well and get along with others and have interpersonal skills, the giftedness is great, but you can't be in a little cell all by yourself the rest of your life, thinking, *Isn't it great that I know all of this information and knowledge!*"

Then Zobelein began to speak about a few exceptional examples of teaching in junior high school. She stated, "I had one year where I taught junior high. One of my students was quite rambunctious and misbehaving. I really worked with her to try and turn this around and get her more focused, and she made some progress. So one night at home, I decided I would call her mother and tell her how pleased I was with the progress of her daughter. So when the mother picked up the phone, I said, 'This is Jennifer Zobelein calling, and I'm your daughter's teacher.' She almost hung up because she was so used to having her daughter in trouble. I said, 'No, no, don't hang up. I want to tell you something good.' So I told her how I had been working with her daughter and how she had definitely improved, and I just wanted her to know that. Well, the mother was in tears. She said, 'Nobody, no teacher, has ever called me to tell me something good about my daughter.' So I realized how important positive reinforcement is. It's much better than punishment, whether it's parenting or teaching, and how important that is in all aspects of our lives. Whether we're a student or we're a grown-up member of society, this positive reinforcement of others, whether it's family or friends or neighbors or coworkers, makes such a difference."

Zobelein went on to say how critically important the home life and family support is to the success of a student's education. She said that for a young student to be successful it takes a village of supporters, such as the mother, father, and the family unit, along with the village of academia. The village of academia would be the teachers, principals, and counselors.

During her teaching career, many of her experiences took her to places that were unexpected. Zobelein explained that part of her time was spent with the Juvenile Detention Center in Oxnard, California, where she taught with many other volunteers. Their major goal while tutoring these detainees was to assist them to pass the GED, which is the equivalent of a high school degree. She stated that it was very fulfilling to teach these young adults, since through the creative writing process, many of these juvenile detainees, since they were incarcerated, had very interesting and difficult life stories to tell. She said that it helped them to deal with the ordeals that they had to endure in their lives, and writing their essays became cathartic and provided relief. Zobelein said that creative writing was, for this population, a very healing process.

In summary, she made these comments: "During the last fifty years, I have seen that my knowledge of the English language has been critical in multiple ways. I have applied these skills in so many areas: reading and understanding contracts, as well as writing them; making contracts for personal loans, for film distribution agreements, for the employment of a conductor and an executive director to run a symphony. I even found myself negotiating a new contract with the musicians under labor union rules, things that I never expected to be doing when I was in college because you don't know where life will lead you. For instance, there is such a diversity of organizations that actually benefit from the use of bylaws, and somebody has to write them, and they have to be written clearly. Then it is important to be able to explain them, making sure they're appropriate to the government of the organization, or to the symphony orchestra, or the congregation of the church for which they are intended. Of course, writing letters and reports and addressing complex issues in a way that is clear and concise is important, as well as conveying information in a diplomatic manner that can be persuasive because you have some points you want to communicate; using words that are descriptive and interesting and not boring; resolving controversies with calm persuasion. All of these are important skills.

"Creative writing is a lot of fun because you get to produce something that hasn't been written before—even in ways that you wouldn't have thought of, like writing a special letter to someone who's done something for you that's very meaningful. In a quick text message, you might say,

'Thank you so much. I appreciate your help.' But to be able to write something that really expresses your gratitude for what that person has done is far more meaningful. For instance, when I had cataract surgery on my eyes, I wrote a poem about what that meant to me, how my vision had improved, and sent it to the doctor who did the surgery. He was just overwhelmed by the fact that I would take the time to do that and send it to him, and it meant so much more than just a quick thank you saying, 'Now, I can see where I couldn't before.'"

Giving and Serving Others Creates Great Joy in Life—The Zobelein Principle of Philanthropy

As we finalize Zobelein's interview, she ends with a discussion of her philanthropic work. It is soon very apparent that philanthropy is certainly one of the highlights of her life. Throughout her life, she has always given to others, whether in teaching, writing and through all types of communication, or by making financial contributions. Another one of her true passions is her love of music. In her adult life, Zobelein was able to combine philanthropy with music through the New West Symphony located in Thousand Oaks, California. Zobelein described her experience with the New West Symphony as follows: "It is the only professional orchestra in Ventura County, and the interesting thing is that my husband and I got involved because we love good music. I had a music minor in college, and my husband is a musician (performer and composer). Music is a passion of ours. We began contributing to the symphony, and the more we got involved, the more we realized the New West Symphony was in deep financial trouble, on the verge of bankruptcy."

As Zobelein began to understand the dire financial situation of the New West Symphony, she saw the need to take on a leadership role within the organization. She said, "You hear people say, 'Put your money where your mouth is.' But it's also true in reverse. Put your mouth where your money is. If you see something of value that you want to contribute to and you're willing to give money or time to support it, then you should also back that up with supportive words and communication, verbal and written, to convince other people and persuade them that this is a good cause. Or, you might serve on a board or committee. So we began doing that. Well eventually, I ended up being the president of the symphony because I kept asking all kinds of questions about the organization. So I realized there was a great need for business skills, not just communication skills, and that we needed a finance committee." Zobelein said, "I'm willing to be president only if you put a finance committee in place."

Again, during the interview, I was incredibly impressed by the leadership, communication, business administration, and persuasion skills that Zobelein possessed in order to have the courage and confidence to take on a tremendously important role as the New West Symphony president. She also had the business knowledge and experience to understand that having a new finance committee in place would be paramount for turning around this symphony's financial condition. Zobelein continued, "We monitored the cash flow. The committee gave reports to the board. We began to project income and expenses, because there wasn't anything dishonest going on before. The prior administration had just allowed the debts to pile up." I noted that, after all, this was a business, and she responded by saying, "It is. A third of the symphony's income is from ticket sales, but you have to raise the other two-thirds—and it's like PBS, you cannot ever let up. You have to always be asking for financial support because you are maintaining something of value. So you need the communication skills to persuade people of the value, but you need the business skills to get the financial support that you need, whether it's individual patrons or a corporate sponsorship or wherever the money is coming from. So I found, again, you need to be a good communicator. You have to have a passion for what you're doing, be a good administrator, overseeing staff as well as musicians, understanding marketing, promotion, and have the gift for fundraising. All of those things are part of what it takes to not only make this business survive but also to flourish!"

New West Symphony President: Negotiations of New Contracts

During the interview, I noted the tremendous responsibility that she had as the president of the New West Symphony. She described that not only did she have the responsibility of raising funds and putting the organization on a sound financial foundation, but she also had to act as a dispute resolution arbitrator in order to renegotiate new contracts, as well as look for a new conductor. These were quite daunting tasks, especially given the fact that they had to be done concurrently.

Zobelein explained the nature of the negotiations. "Through this whole process of taking over a whole symphony orchestra, we were in the middle of negotiations with the labor union, the American Federation of Musicians. Their contract was expiring, so it needed to be renegotiated, and I had never done that before, but I knew that there had to be a common ground because in the past, it had been really confrontational. It was the administration against the musicians, and there was a very negative culture in place. But my husband and I, being musicians, had become friendly with a lot of the musicians in the orchestra, and they knew that we respected them. So going into these negotiations, it was with a different frame of reference because there was mutual respect. They even trusted me to write down all the notes from our meetings because I was the communicator. I put all of the changes in the contract as we discussed them, and of course they confirmed the changes afterwards. The musicians had to take a pay cut, which is not easy to negotiate, but due to our mutual trust, they accepted the new contract with pay raises given later. Over the long term, the musicians would be making more each year to bring their annual pay back to the standard rate." Zobelein continued, "We worked out a mutually satisfactory agreement, and at the annual meeting of ACSO (Association of California Symphony Orchestras), a New York labor union representative was there speaking about musicians' contracts, and he actually complimented New West Symphony, commenting on its excellent negotiations with the musicians, in front of an audience of hundreds of people."

She felt quite honored by these words spoken by the New York union representative and mentioned again that communication skills, both spoken and written, were of vital importance during these negotiations. She also said that to be able to see the opinion of the other side and to respect each other was equally important during this dispute resolution. Zobelein commented that it was an extremely satisfying and rewarding event in her life.

Virginia Gean, MBA, CMA

New West Symphony: Hiring a New Conductor

Another responsibility that Zobelein had to undertake in her role as president of the New West Symphony was finding a new conductor. She marvels at their good fortune, since they were able to find a remarkably young and talented conductor from Brazil. His name was Marcelo Lehninger, and he expressed amazing artistry in his conducting and music selections. She described the previous conductor's personality as more authoritarian—a much more "old school" mentality that the musicians did not appreciate. This was unlike the personality of the new Brazilian conductor. "Marcelo Lehninger, our new conductor, was much more collegial, and this style works better with the musicians because there is a mutual respect there, and he can correct them in a very kind way, so they don't feel insulted, and they love working for him. You can just see the passion and the joy. It was not just a job for the new conductor. The musicians were enjoying the new style of leadership of Marcelo Lehninger, and that made a huge difference."

Zobelein and her staff interviewed six different conductors for this upcoming position, and they all came to the same conclusion that Mr. Lehninger would be the best fit as the conductor for the New West Symphony. "Well, we had a committee. We had two musicians from the orchestra, board members from each of our three regions: Ventura, Thousand Oaks, and Santa Monica. We needed somebody from staff, so our executive director and all of us went through rehearsals, watching them perform, seeing the interaction between the guest conductor and the musicians and then interviewing each of them. It was an amazing process. It was a unanimous decision that Marcelo was the one that just met all of those criteria. We had a list of things we were looking for. We're always looking for new ideas, and Marcelo is wonderful at that because he has a different approach to programming than in the past, and it's been very successful. This is now his fourth season." Zobelein commented that they have been incredibly proud of his success as a conductor, and as he became better known to the audience, ticket sales increased, further improving cash flow and stability for the financial health of the New West Symphony.

A Village of Knowledge

Left to right: Jennifer and Craig Zobelein displaying the book, *A Forest of Pipes*, and their *Walt Disney Concert Hall Organ* documentary. In front of an appreciation plaque presented to Jennifer at the Walt Disney Concert Hall in May 2012. Jennifer Zobelein seated for the documentary videography screening Q&A session.

Jennifer Zobelein—Forest of Pipes

In 2004, Jennifer and her husband attended the inaugural concert of the pipe organ at the Walt Disney Concert Hall in Los Angeles, California. They were enthralled, and Jennifer decided that she would research the history of this beautiful instrument and write a book about it. Zobelein described this wonderful musical project: "After experiencing the visual and tonal impact of the pipe organ at the Walt Disney Concert Hall, I decided to write a book about its design and construction. Originally published in 2007, it is entitled *A Forest of Pipes*. (www.aforestofpipes.com). The 2014 edition was revised for the tenth anniversary of the organ installation and updated with additional information and photos." A few years later, she became the co-executive producer of the premiere recording of the Walt Disney Concert Hall organ, *First and Grand*, released as a CD in 2010 with Christoph Bull as the organist. Dr. Bull is professor of organ at UCLA. Later, Jennifer and her husband coproduced a documentary on the Walt Disney Concert Hall pipe organ. It is in a DVD format with a bonus CD of additional music played by ten well-known organists. It is a fascinating story, brought to life through interviews, music, and exceptional videography (www.disneyhallorgan.com).

Jennifer Zobelein, turning a personal idea into a business idea, *A Forest of Pipes* book signing. On her left is Manuel Rosales, the tonal designer of the organ. On her right is Caspar Glatter-Gotz, German organ builder.

Jennifer Zobelein's Philosophy on Life

As Zobelein begins to reflect on her life, there are a few guiding principles that lead her. She mentions her nature of being risk averse in financial terms. Having been raised during World War II, conservative values regarding money, investments, and risk management are important to

A Village of Knowledge

her. She strongly believes that being fiscally conservative is a virtue that leads to a blessed and stable life. Zobelein contrasts that with the current younger generations who have leveraged themselves with too much debt, which often leads to personal anguish and heartbreak amongst families. She also sees a correlation with those values to the current state of our United States economy as being risky and foolish, with a deficit of trillions of dollars that will only hurt the future generations of Americans. She feels that this type of behavior both on an individual and a government basis is deeply disturbing.

Zobelein continued by saying, "We grew up in a generation where you didn't go into debt. If you couldn't afford it, you didn't buy it. Especially growing up during World War II, it didn't make any sense to do that, so you would save up for something first and then spend. But now we have a government that is unwilling to cut when you know there is so much waste. You can't keep spending money you don't really have, and you can't go more and more into debt, whether it's a person or a government." She mentions that the individuals living at University Village, her home base, have invested well, and she and her husband have a diversified portfolio that is providing income into the future. On the whole, the individuals who live at University Village have managed risk well.

Zobelein also stresses the importance of the younger generation to seek job opportunities that mirror their passion. She strongly believes in the following philosophy: "You have to be realistic and ask yourself what it is you really like to do. What am I good at doing? What could I do well and be happy in a job that I may have for fifteen to twenty years? Or, you need to be very adaptable and have many different jobs, and maybe with this generation, that may be the way it goes, because in the old days, a lot of people stayed with the same company for fifty years, and I don't think that happens anymore. I think, and I've advised my own children this way, you have to choose something that you can honestly enjoy. If you will be dreading going to work every day, why bother? I mean, you should be doing something that's meaningful, that has a value. So pick a major that will give you that knowledge base in a field where you've got to be practical, and there should be jobs available."

During these series of interviews, I grew to have a tremendous respect for Jennifer Zobelein. I sat in awe of her core principles, her set of leadership skills, her drive for philanthropy, and her teaching capabilities and communication skills, both verbal and written. I understand that here is a woman who has been successful on so many levels, in such an elegant and unselfish manner. Jennifer Zobelein truly represents a Renaissance woman, a woman of exemplary attributes and accomplishments.

A List of Jennifer Zobelein's Core Beliefs and Principles

- A personal interest can lead to a business idea.
- We may create a product or take on a project that is very satisfying but does not produce a profit. We do it for love, not money. And we should give it our best efforts.
- We should be practical in our business decisions but also find satisfaction in our employment.
- Don't take a job just because it pays well.
- Young people do better in school when they have family support at home.
- Students must learn to reason at a higher level and develop critical thinking skills.
- For niche books, self-publishing makes more sense than going to an established publisher.
- The business environment has an effect on social behavior.
- Legal decisions at the state and federal level affect people's personal lives.
- Good traits of character and personal ethics do make a difference in the business world.
- Put your money where your mouth is—and also, put your mouth where your money is.

Chapter 7
Peggy Perry, Volunteer, Teacher and Author

Peggy Perry

The Philosophy of a Volunteer: Commit to a Positive Attitude in Life

Be Grateful, Be Happy, and Smile

Fuller Seminary, Author, and Volunteer

As the interview with Peggy Perry begins, it is not long before I realize that she is a true "life coach." This chapter identifies her important life lessons and motivational way of thinking and communicating, which are significant not only on a personal basis but also on a business level. Ms. Perry's personality is vibrant and positive, and her ethical and moral standards are high. As I reflect during her interview, I am struck by the number of lessons she describes. Her words are carefully chosen as she tells her stories. Words such as failure, turtle, cloakroom, chasing dreams, Holland, poems, faith, judge, service, volunteer, nightmares, swimmer, river, horizon, smile queen, parachute, and pearls are delivered with enthusiasm and warmth. Powerful messages become evident, as each word identifies a concept and many metaphors are examined. As this chapter explores the messages of which Peggy Perry so eloquently speaks, you will discover that she is quite the wordsmith.

Early Life and Eliminating the Fear Factor in Life and in Business

Perry describes her early life as quite typical for many women of her generation. "I am a native Southern Californian. My grandparents on both sides settled in Southern California. My parents met at the University of Southern California (USC), so I have the Trojans' cardinal and gold blood. I grew up in Glendale, right over the hill from the Rose Bowl, where my father had been an enthusiastic cheerleader for the USC football team in the 1920s. It was always assumed I would attend USC, and I did. I loved my college experience; in 1948, it was exciting to be in school with all those World War II veterans who were completing their education on the GI Bill. My husband-to-be, Tom, was one of them. He graduated two years ahead of me, and life without him was a little lonely, although I was busy in campus activities. When we decided to be married at the end of my junior year, I told myself and everybody around that I would graduate, which in those days most girls who married before graduation did not. I did! Bachelor's degree in hand, I taught school briefly, which leads me to my next story.

"I would like to talk about failure. Because I think failure is certainly and inevitably going to be a part of one's life. It doesn't really matter when or how it comes. As I reflect on my life, what I see as my biggest failure came when I was twenty-two years old, the year I went to work as an elementary school teacher. That was a long time ago; I am glad I got it behind me early.

"Newly married while I completed my studies at USC, I pushed myself hard. I finished school in August and wanted to start teaching in September.

There weren't a lot of jobs available by the time I graduated. Positions in the nicer communities had already been spoken for by the May graduates. So I started teaching in Los Angeles. Now, in those days, in 1952, you have to remember that everybody in my world looked like me. We were not yet the multicultural society we are today, where our grandchildren have grown up not even thinking about visible and cultural differences between them and their friends and other contemporaries. We all were 'the same.' But Los Angeles did not look like me, and I really didn't know how to deal with that. It probably wasn't the neighborhood, although you have to be able to teach in ways that the children can learn, and maybe I wasn't doing that. Whatever the reason, I did not do well in the classroom.

"My principal said to me at one point, 'Peggy, I have never had anyone come into my school with higher recommendations than you brought from your university experience. And I've never had anyone fail as miserably.' Now, that was nice, wasn't it? But he was right. I was just a total failure. I didn't know how to put together a curriculum. I didn't know how to put together a day's work, a week's work. I couldn't control the children. My gosh, I started with the second grade, and then the principal put me into a combination third-and fourth-grade classroom. He bounced me around, so I was always doing something different and new, which probably didn't help either. However, that was no excuse. I just wasn't doing my job. I didn't want to go to work. In fact, many mornings I felt really sick.

"One day I realized, oh, my goodness, I know what's going on! Not many days later, a sweet little second grader told me, 'Ooooo, Mz. Perry, you gonna git a baby!' I was, and I did, one month after my minimum year of teaching ended. My teaching ended in May, and my firstborn, David, arrived in June, which might have had something to do with my failure in the classroom."

Nightmares about Failure

"Nevertheless, I continued to have nightmares about all of the children being lined up out in the playground for a fire drill, which we had in those days. In my dream, everybody else's classes were lined up and orderly; my kids were running around everywhere, and I had no control. It was still that horrible sense of failure that I could not overcome. Over time, it has taught me this lesson. You can't always go back and correct a particular problem from the past. You can, however, move on; you can be more sensitive to other people who are having difficulty, who are failing at something; you can look at your successes later and be grateful for them, because you can compare them with that devastating earlier experience. This is particularly true when you are a high achiever, as I have been since I was a child."

Consider the Turtle—It Gets Nowhere Unless It Sticks Its Neck Out

"To me, that was a defining experience and leads me to say to young people, don't be afraid. Consider the turtle. The turtle gets nowhere unless he sticks his neck out! So my recommendation is go ahead, explore different opportunities that come your way. I think young people today are receiving more of this advice. Try it, try something new, and don't expect to be successful the first time. Keep trying new things. Broaden your horizon and try to get past failure as quickly as you can and move on to the next success. That's one thing I want to emphasize."

As I was listening to Peggy Perry's advice, I remembered the many different stories of successes and failures of those individuals I had interviewed. Many had the same advice, that one should try different strategies for a career, and if you do not at first succeed in a position, try and try again in other occupations that might interest you.

Chase Whatever Dreams You Dare to Dream and the Beauty of the Spiral

"I feel strongly about choosing the things that you do with your life. I believe we should, as much as we can (sometimes through not just ourselves but through other people's feedback, too) identify the things that we do best, perhaps better than most people. Do them. If you can, isolate those characteristics, those interests, that training, that experience you have had—all those things that make you a little bit different from other people. Then concentrate on developing that uniqueness. When you know that you can do something well, why not do that?" In other words, Ms. Perry was suggesting that you realize your competitive advantage. "I think that becomes not only the best use of your time," she continued, "but it also is what's going to give you the greatest sense of fulfillment. And, by embracing experiences that enable you to do well, you will get even better at anything you do.

"On the other hand, I also strongly believe in chasing whatever dreams that you dare to dream. Starting out, many people simply do not know what they want to do on a professional basis. So try those things that interest you, intrigue you. At the beginning, you may not do your best, even when you try. I have to admit that I often don't try new things if I don't think I can do them well. We all want to excel; no one wants to fail. I think I grew up being successful in what I did, because I tried only the things at which I thought I'd be successful! Maybe that is too limiting. Be patient with yourself and stay flexible.

"I do believe that whatever path we choose, we don't learn in a straight line or in a circle. I believe life is a spiral, in which that line moves forward and upward." I thought Ms. Perry's philosophy was an interesting commentary on becoming a better person by doing what you do best. Instead of a straight line or a circle, it takes more of an oscillating or spiral shape upward.

Do Those Things That Come from Your Heart and the Importance of Volunteering

"The heart of me is volunteerism. I believe don't always do things just for the almighty dollar but find those things that come from your heart. Because of my Christian faith, it's been easy for me. Many of the things I've done with my time have been associated with the church. The Bible study that I have taught recently is nondenominational and reaches out to people whether or not they are believers. One of my main purposes in life is to share the good news, the Christian gospel, with them. The things that define me may not define somebody else. But whatever it is that interests you, find a place that you can use it. Volunteer at a pet clinic or a soup kitchen, or go with a group like Habitat for Humanity and help build a house if you like hammers and nails and saws. Follow your heart and find a place that you can do something that interests you for the good of other people. For me, that brings the greatest satisfaction of all in life."

As I thought of the marvelous message that Perry was conveying, I agreed that helping and serving others gives life greater meaning. Indeed, this was wonderful advice. I recalled her sense of failure in that classroom and the stress that must have brought in her life. I asked her if, when she was twenty-two years old, she wanted to make herself a better person, and was part of her journey to discover how volunteering and serving others brought great joy in life. She responded, "I don't know. I was just so down. It took me some time to put myself together. Actually, no, I didn't have much time! First of all, we moved into a home; we had just bought our first house. So when I stopped teaching, we'd been married for two years. I was on my way to becoming a homeowner at age twenty-two. I had to learn to keep house. And to take care of my husband, of course, in the ways wives do. And within a month, I became a mom. So, no, I didn't have very much time for self-pity. I just had time for nightmares when nobody else was looking. And they still come back sometimes. Well, other things have certainly superseded that!

"After that one year of teaching, I took about fifteen years to produce and raise a family of four children." I asked about her children. "We had three boys and one girl. My daughter was third and was born on New Year's Eve. Oh, my, what a gift! Then, three years later, along came Steve. So, four children in six and a half years. I actually had four teenagers at one period, for six months.

"About the time the two older ones were into high school, my husband said, 'We have a lot of kids here heading for college. Could you help, please?' So I went to work at Fuller Theological Seminary in Pasadena. That wasn't much help in financing the college education; you don't work for a church-related educational institution like that and make much money. But it was a very interesting and rewarding experience. I had four different responsibilities, beginning as a secretary in the development department, then helping establish a doctor of ministry program as an administrative assistant to the director and, later, raising financial support for the seminary as the alumni director. My final position was director of student housing. Not too many people at University Village know that I managed four hundred units of student housing, but I did." When I asked Perry how many years she worked at the seminary, she responded, "Ten years."

Continuing to Serve Others through the Real Estate Profession

Since she enjoyed working with student housing, Perry considered going into property management professionally after leaving Fuller. But she soon learned that you either had to own the company (which she really didn't want to do) or you had to start at ground level (she said she was far too old and sassy to put up with that).

"After I passed my real estate exam and looked at property management opportunities, I decided not to go in that direction. Sometimes we make mistakes. So, licensed as a Realtor, I decided to see how it would feel to buy and sell houses, and I joined a local residential real estate company. I quickly determined that I was not buying and selling houses; I was helping other people buy and sell their homes. That was a vast difference. I especially enjoyed helping young first-time buyers." Perry considered her work a service to others, not strictly a commercial, income-producing proposition. "I never could have supported a family on the money I earned in my ten-year real estate career," she said, "but I had a lot of fun giving myself away. And my commissions did help put those kids through college!"

Through real estate, Perry was able to open herself to the world of business after spending a lifetime in the nonprofit, education, and volunteer arenas. "I was having totally different experiences in life that I might never have had otherwise, particularly in real estate. I had never been associated with business. I'd been in the world of education and the church, often as a volunteer. So real estate had me opening the business pages of the newspaper and watching what was happening in the stock market and in the economy in general. In my late fifties, I was learning business principles, particularly salesmanship—although I resisted the concept of 'selling real estate' because to me it was always an act of service."

I commented that she probably was a better agent for having core principles of serving others and that others would recognize this effective leadership quality. "It's what made it effective for me, but that may not be true for everybody. Certainly this is a critical component of the values of my life." I responded that I thought by serving others and the needs of their customers, more businesses would become more successful. Perry commented, "I would hope so, but I don't think it's always true. No, I think many people are motivated purely by money and whatever it takes to make it. I don't think that makes it right, and it certainly doesn't make it right for me. But I don't want to judge others."

Retirement Brings New Challenges

Perry moved on, describing the next phase of her life. "Then I began to retire from my so-called business career because, at that point, my husband was developing the symptoms of Alzheimer's disease, and I needed to be at home with him. He was self-employed and had worked from home for many years, but that didn't last much longer. We did travel during that time, particularly during the last few years of the ten that I worked as a Realtor. In that period, both Tom and I controlled our own schedules (an entrepreneurial benefit!), and we took some nice trips. They were usually a week or two; three weeks was the maximum, with one exception when our youngest son was married in India. We continued to travel, even as his Alzheimer's developed. I simply told our traveling companions and our tour guides what our situation was, and they were marvelously supportive as we continued to live the good life."

She reflected back to a time and an event that brought about a big change in her life. "One Sunday, a tree fell down in our front yard. I asked a friend to come after church and help me cut it into pieces. As he sawed the tree, and I dumped pieces into the trash barrels, my husband was inside but, of course, not able to help either of us. I said to my friend, 'Bob, I think I'm going to have to find someplace else to live, because I can't keep calling on my friends to help like this.' Do-it-yourselfer that I was, I never thought of calling in a professional; we had always done house and garden maintenance ourselves. Anyway, Bob said that he and his wife had found a wonderful community for our stage of life—in Thousand Oaks, near where our daughter and her family were living in Moorpark. One thing led to another, and within the month, I had signed up for UVTO (University Village Thousand Oaks). What a blessing that has been!"

I asked Perry how long ago that was. "Let's see. That was 2004, before ground had been broken. This was just a grassy plain out here, with a stream running through it, and there was nothing but a sales trailer on the land. I moved in during August of 2007, one of the first forty residents." It sounded as if she has loved living at University Village among many interesting neighbors. Currently, there are five hundred residents in the independent living community (which has a two-year wait list), with more in OakView, the on-campus skilled nursing and assisted living residence. Perry said that she has made many wonderful friends living there.

Life at University Village and Memories of the Cloakroom

Two years after Perry's husband was placed in residential care for Alzheimer's, University Village was ready for its occupants. OakView had not been built, so he spent the final year of his life about fifty miles away, with Perry visiting him twice a week. Alone, Perry reinvented her life, tapping into her heart as she plunged into all that her new home offered. She made a big commitment to writing for the monthly, on-campus newspaper published by the Activities Department, and she says, "Here I have become 'the person who writes those articles.' I've always enjoyed writing, though I never did it professionally. I can remember being sent, as a child, to the cloakroom. 'Cloakroom.' That dates me, doesn't it? It opened onto our classroom, and it was where we kept sweaters and lunchboxes—unused and quiet, though a bit dark, during the school day. I was probably nine years old. I had finished my assignments while most of the class still worked, and I asked the teacher what I should do next, adding that I thought I'd like to write a poem. 'Go in the cloakroom and write,' she suggested. My third-grade class was studying Holland, and in some magazine I had seen a poem that inspired me. So, using some unknown author's idea, I wrote my first masterpiece: *Skies and seas all shades of blues, children playing in wooden shoes.* Several stanzas followed, and then the 'inspired' ending, *Yes, this is Holland.* From then on, when I had finished my work with time to spare, I went to the cloakroom, ultimately producing a book of poems, which I lovingly copied for my grandmother. The book cover was made of yucca fiber, tied with leather thongs. When my grandmother died, my mother retrieved my book, and now I have it. That was the beginning of my love of writing, I guess.

"When clubs were first established at UVTO, I was the only one who was interested in a Newsletter Club for the Activities Department. So I helped write what was at that time a sixteen-page paper, which has been cut back to eight pages. Now, eight years later, I still write for that monthly paper, *Village View*, and also help with the weekly bulletin of announcements, *University Update*. And I have enjoyed so many other ways of contributing to life in this new home. I've served on committees, often as secretary (guess why!), and on the Resident Council (our residents' governing body). And too many projects and responsibilities to list! Many involve writing—like the Bible study I led for almost three years, which meant writing a four-page lesson every week! That was particularly rewarding for me because I depended on materials that I was trained to use four decades ago. It was wonderful to get into those forty lessons and share them once again. But the people here are the best part, so interesting and so supportive."

The Importance of Smiling and the Professional Needle Poker

"Meeting new people—that reminds me of a decision I made when I was a freshman at USC. The first day of school, I walked out of the dorm to go to class. I thought, *All right, I am going to meet a lot of people walking down this sidewalk toward me, people I've never seen before. Maybe someday I will get to know them, maybe I won't. So what will I do?* A lot of people walk along with their heads down, looking at the sidewalk. But I decided, *No, I won't do that. I am going look at people, and smile.* Thanks to my parents and my orthodontist, I have an okay smile. Well, God had something to do with it, too. Whatever, I decided to use it.

"For the rest of my life, I have tried to smile. Physiologically, it makes you feel better. There is something about those muscles in your cheeks, pulling upward, that heightens the spirits as well the expression on your face. So, smile!" I asked Perry, what is it about the smile that you think helps connect people? Why has God blessed us with smiling, and why is that important? Perry responded, "First of all, it says that you are not an adversary. It also means that you have the potential, at least, of being a friend. I don't know why smiles connect us, but they do. When you travel the world, it's the smiles of other people that connect and make us feel that there are no boundaries between us. We are all people. We all have feelings. For the moment, at least, we choose 'up' feelings, rather than 'down.' And 'back and forth' feelings join us together. I think that's what a smile does. It connects us to a person. It makes us feel like yeah, we're in sync. It says, 'You are okay. Whatever you are about to say next, it is okay—at least until you say it!'"

I commented, but you could see someone who is not able to communicate in your language, and you see them smiling. Children do it all the time. "Oh, yes," Perry responded. "Isn't it fun to walk through a mall, and somebody comes by with a baby, and you look at that baby and smile? When it responds with a smile, what joy! Absolute joy. I have great-grandbabies now. Talk about smiles and joy!

"Again, a salesperson in a store smiles at you when she says, 'Is there something I can do to help?' Then she smiles like she really means it. She may have been taught to do it; that's okay. It's still a smile, and smiles are contagious, not only with other people but within ourselves. Once we make it a habit, it becomes a way of life, something we become, when we consciously decide to smile, as I did that day at USC. If you are selling, throw a smile in with your sales pitch. It doesn't have to be phony. If you are giving service to another person, smile, even if you are poking him in the arm with a needle. If you smile, chances are it won't hurt as much, and that must be the goal of the professional needle poker."

Perry again recalls her university days. "They had a contest for the Hello and Smile Queen. I always thought I should win it, but I never did. The girls who won had good smiles but better bodies than I had, but what did that have to do with their smiles? So I never had that lovely title, but I considered myself a hello and smile queen anyway!" During our interview, Perry continues to display her beautiful smile, which is truly infectious!

Reflections on the River and Choosing the Right Path

Nearing the end of our interview, Perry related what she called a profound experience from years past. "While my young family was vacationing in Sequoia, I had a moment of quiet, sitting on this rock by a little creek, looking at the water tumbling down. I was feeling philosophical while my husband kept an eye on the four kids. I thought, *This creek is a metaphor for life. You really can choose the kind of path you want to follow. You can go into those little eddies along the edge of the stream, where it's quiet among the rocks and the rushes and the bubbles and maybe the fish. It would be a peaceful life; you probably wouldn't have too much that ruffled you. But look out in the middle, where it's moving, where it's going somewhere. That's the place where you get tossed along over the rocks. That's where the rough edges get smoothed off, and sometimes that's going to hurt. Some of those rocks are pretty jagged. But that's the challenging life, the life I want. That's where I want to be, not in the quiet pools along the side but out in the middle, even if it might be painful.* So that's the way I've lived, and sometimes I got hurt. And sometimes I have hurt other people, which I never intended to do. When that happens, I try to go to them and apologize. Then my body heals, and my mind heals, and my spirit heals. That's good! And it gives me the courage to stay out there."

I responded, when you are in the middle of the river, you can be a cork or a swimmer, and you have chosen to be a swimmer. Perry agreed. "Yes, I choose to be a swimmer in life, not a cork just bobbing up and down. Even a strong swimmer sometimes will be carried along by a strong current. You use your swimming skills, and sometimes you have to head for the quiet spots. You can't stay out in the center all the time, I guess. As I get older, I find it's harder and harder to be there continuously, as I used to like it. But I still prefer the current to the quiet."

I asked if she had ever kayaked in white water, and she responded, "Not kayaking, but I have done some white-water rafting. Sometimes you come to rapids, with various degrees of difficulty to navigate. When they are dangerous, more difficult than the passengers' degree of proficiency, the leader says, 'Get out of the boat and carry it around the rapids.' You don't argue; you carry the boat! You have to acknowledge your capabilities, your experience. Then you turn to your source of guidance, whatever that is. In my case, it might be prayer, and it might be some practical information. Or it might simply be talking to a guide who knows more than I do. If that source responds, 'Get out of the boat,' I get out and carry it. I don't go through the dangerous rapids or over the falls. I think that's a good metaphor, too."

Perry had one last contribution. "There is another thing to remember. If you don't know where you are going, you will probably end up somewhere else. That's from *What Color Is Your Parachute?* by Richard Bolles. It's not new, but it's a good statement, and the book is a great manual for job hunters and career changers."

As we ended our time together, I expressed my appreciation and awe of her wisdom. Perry said, "Maybe I got wise in my old age. Or maybe it came from my parents and grandparents. I don't know. Wisdom usually comes with age, though I guess some people are wise sooner in life than others. Knowledge and sharing other people's experiences can come from the beginning, so listen to a wise person for that reason. You may not want to follow their advice, but if you tuck it away somewhere, it might do some good, some time."

I continued to be awestruck by the philosophy of Ms. Peggy Perry, and I knew deep down in my heart that these thoughts and metaphors that she described would, indeed, be wise stories to pass on to others.

Acknowledgements

This book could never have been completed without assisted contributions of an inestimable value from a number of individuals. We express to them our most sincere gratitude for their generous help and support of every kind.

Dr. Gerhard Apfelthaler, Dean of the CLU School of Management, had the vision to direct Virginia Gean to the Thousand Oaks University Village of residents. Knowing of her keen interest in both business and people combined with her conversational skills, the dean had confidence that a project such as this could be taken from concept to completion.

We are extremely grateful for the role Blaine Shull played in selecting the best interviewees and planning and organizing the taped interviews. His attention to details and his people skills were so critical.

Harriet Young, Virginia's mother, is owed a big debt of appreciation for her unfailing eye as she read all the manuscripts carefully for grammar and syntax changes. The benefits of her suggestions, constant support and encouragement played a significant role in the final product.

Grateful praise is extended to each of the interviewees for their unselfishness in taking time to share their stories. They artfully shared their wealth of experience, and vast wisdom with a tremendous degree of enthusiasm.

To Teri Watkins of AuthorHouse we are especially indebted for shepherding this writing through all aspects of this production.

We also thank the owners of the Thousand Oaks University Village for allowing us to freely access the residents and providing encouragement and helpful ideas along the way.

About the Authors

Virginia Gean, MBA, CMA

Virginia Gean is a lecturer at the School of Management of California Lutheran University. She has been a member of the faculty for the past thirteen years. She is popular among the MBA, undergraduate, and professional students at CLU where she teaches accounting and finance.

Prior to joining the CLU faculty and in keeping with the entrepreneurial spirit of her family, she founded and managed her own apparel business for fifteen years. Her business was manufacturing women's business suits and was marketed under the brand name Vergianni. She eventually sold this business, and proceeds were invested into commercial real estate in California and South Carolina. She enjoys being an investor in real estate as well as other ventures, which includes a nursery, growing flowering plants in industrial hothouses. Her wealth of experience from being an entrepreneur enriches her classroom performance for students.

She has published numerous scholarly papers in peer-reviewed journals. She has made numerous professional presentations at both national and international business conferences. She was selected to be the keynote speaker at the ASBBS international conference in 2017. The female interviewees included in *A Village of Knowledge* were featured in her keynote address.

Virginia Gean is passionate about business. *A Village of Knowledge* contains stories about great business leaders that are educational, inspiring, and thought provoking, surely to entertain and enlighten future generations.

Farrell Gean, PhD, MBA, CPA, CMA

Dr. Gean is the Luckman Distinguished Professor of Accounting at Pepperdine University in Malibu, California. Completion of the spring semester in 2018 marked thirty-seven academic years as a member of the business administration faculty at Pepperdine. He has also served as an adjunct faculty member in the MBA program for the School of Management at California Lutheran University since 1997.

He was a member of the audit staff of Ernst & Ernst international public accounting firm in Nashville, Tennessee, office prior to joining the Pepperdine faculty in 1981. His consulting experience over the years has focused on the preparation of pro forma financial statements as part of business plans. His clients include internationally known figures such as the late Baron Edmond de Rothschild. His consulting has taken him all over the globe, including such cities as Tokyo, Singapore, Hong Kong, Riyadh, Bali, Cancun, London, Zurich, Frankfurt, New Deli, Dunedin, and Beijing. He has published numerous articles in scholarly peer-reviewed journals and has made formal presentations in the United States at international conferences from Maui to Manhattan.

He is an avid golfer. He was inducted into the Lipscomb University Athletics Hall of Fame in November 2011 as the last player of two sports, baseball and basketball, over a four year period.

CPSIA information can be obtained
at www.ICGtesting.com
Printed in the USA
BVHW03s0758231018
530986BV00001B/15/P